Leeds Town Hall, designed by Cuthbert Broderick (1858).

Shire County Guide 21

WEST YORKSHIRE

Colin Speakman

Shire Publications Ltd

CONTENTS

1. The heart of the old West Riding 3
2. The countryside 5
3. Archaeological sites 11
4. Castles and monastic ruins 14
5. Churches 16
6. Historic houses and gardens 20
7. Museums and galleries 25
8. Industrial history 32
9. Canals and railways 35
10. Famous people 39
11. Towns and villages 41
12. Getting around 53
13. Tourist information centres 53

Map of West Yorkshire 54

Index 56

 First published 1988. Shire County Guide 21. ISBN 0 85263 936 8.

Printed in Great Britain by C. I. Thomas & Sons (Haverfordwest) Ltd, Press Buildings, Merlins Bridge, Haverfordwest, Dyfed SA61 1XF.

British Library Cataloguing in Publication Data: Speakman, Colin. *West Yorkshire.* Shire County Guide; v. 21. 1. Yorkshire (Metropolitan County) Visitors' guides. I. Title. 914. 28'104858. ISBN 0-85263-936-8.

ACKNOWLEDGEMENTS

This book could not have been written without the very considerable help and detailed research of Lydia Speakman. Needless to say, any mistakes are my own.

The photograph on page 21 is reproduced by kind permission of the *Yorkshire Post* and *Yorkshire Evening Post*, Leeds. The photographs on pages 5, 7, 42, 48 and 51 are by Colin Speakman. All other photographs, including the front cover, are by Cadbury Lamb. The map is by D. R. Darton.

Cover: *The Cloth Hall Tower in Ravensknowle Park, Huddersfield.*

Below: *Leeds Civic Hall, dating from the 1930s.*

Riders at Adwalton Moor, scene of a Civil War battle in 1643, when the Royalist army defeated the Parliamentarians.

1
The heart of the old West Riding

West Yorkshire is not an old county in bureaucratic terms. It was created only in 1974 out of the vast old West Riding of Yorkshire, that mighty expanse of Pennine England that stretched from the English Midlands to the Lake District and almost to the Scottish Border Country. And it ceased to exist as an administrative unit on 1st April 1986, when, as part of further sweeping changes to local government in England and Wales, the new metropolitan counties, including West Yorkshire, were abolished. This left the five metropolitan districts of Leeds, Bradford, Calderdale, Kirklees and Wakefield to form the loose collective of local authorities which now constitutes the County of West Yorkshire.

Little wonder, therefore, that many people in West Yorkshire, including some of the local authorities themselves, now prefer to use the name 'West Riding' for their region, with its memories of rugged independence and character dating back to Saxon times, when England's largest county was divided into thirds or 'thriddings' (hence Ridings).

The old West Riding was, however, far bigger than modern West Yorkshire. West Yorkshire is West Riding topped and tailed: the top being the superb gritstone and limestone landscapes of the Yorkshire Dales, which have now passed to North Yorkshire (and even into Cumbria), the tail being the iron and steel country of Barnsley, Rotherham and Sheffield, which now forms an entirely separate county, South Yorkshire.

So West Yorkshire is the core, the heart and, many people would feel, the very soul of the old West Riding. It includes most of the largest towns and cities (Leeds, Wakefield, Bradford, Halifax, Huddersfield), the great woollen and clothing manufacturing centres that are synonymous with Yorkshire and Yorkshireness throughout the world. It also includes much of that very special landscape (the Brontë Moors, the Pennine valleys, the mill towns), so familiar through films and television. But West Yorkshire is not just about a romanticised past, as any civic hall inspired brochure will remind you. West Yorkshire also means progress, new factories, modern industry, motorways, a newly expanded airport, new trains, bustling prosperity and enterprise.

A sense of history

In West Yorkshire the deeply rooted presence of the past is all around. You cannot wander the moors without being aware of the long struggle against untamed nature on those high moorland farms, the endless, snow-bound winters, the late, cold springs, the all too brief summers. In an area like the Pennines man never wholly conquers a hostile environment, merely comes to terms with it. You cannot walk through any small West Yorkshire town without seeing the evidence of the industrialisation of Britain: that tremendous release

of creative energy and enterprise which, in the North of England, produced the world's first industrial economy and laid the basis for all Britain's subsequent economic and political power.

A people of character

The people of the county shaped this landscape and have been deeply influenced by it. It has been said that a Yorkshireman or Yorkshirewoman is from Yorkshire first and from England only second: being Yorkshire is almost a question of nationhood. The caricature of the blunt, aggressive, no-nonsense, hardheaded Yorkshireman is an image carefully nurtured by comedians, cricketers and politicians and has grown out of a sliver of truth. Life on the Pennine foothills was never easy, and generations of families who have grown up in a culture dominated by the harsh disciplines of mill life and hard times have had to develop toughness and resilience. But what many visitors to the county have most enjoyed and appreciated about their experience on holiday in the area is the warmth and kindness of the people.

The statue of the Black Prince by Sir Thomas Brock, in City Square, Leeds.

A wintry scene at Stanbury, near Haworth in the Worth Valley.

2
The countryside

An astonishing variety

West Yorkshire has a remarkable variety of countryside within its relatively confined boundaries, from some of the wildest moorland in Britain to flat, agricultural plain, from richly beautiful parkland to heavily urbanised city fringes. However, of all Britain's great industrial areas, West Yorkshire is undoubtedly the 'greenest' in terms of open space: part of one National Park, the Peak District, and the fringe of another, the Yorkshire Dales, and acres of peat and heather moor, farms and pasture, country parks, woods, and, in the towns and cities themselves, superb parks.

The greatest single landscape feature is undoubtedly the Pennines, that massive range of hills, consisting mainly of Carboniferous sandstones and shales, the sandstones of a particularly coarse form known as millstone grit. The Pennines run from central England to Scotland and divide West Yorkshire from neighbouring Lancashire and Greater Manchester, creating a barrier which, in spite of modern communication links, is as much psychological as physical.

For anyone who loves wild country, the Pennines are superbly beautiful. Rising to around 1500 feet (500 metres), they form bleak, almost flat summits, perhaps crowned by a few gritstone crags but more typically consisting of a vast expanse of peat hag, wet boggy land. On the drier slopes heather and bilberry dominate, producing the kind of classic moorland landscape which is richly purple in late summer, the haunt of the red grouse. Each of the great moorland areas is cut through by deep river valleys which begin their lives as steep cloughs or gulleys in the peat bog, soon forming the characteristic Pennine gill (often misspelt 'ghyll' on maps), where rowan and birch trees flourish around a moorland waterfall.

This is classic fell-walking country, a landscape where you can get the smoke and fumes of the city out of your lungs and enjoy the sense of wide, almost limitless horizons, the cry of the curlew or the soaring trill of the skylark. Much of this is water catchment area: the rambler will often come across great moorland reservoirs and their associated dams, catchwaters and tracks. The Yorkshire Water Authority, the principal authority in the management of many of these moorlands, has a liberal attitude to the well behaved rambler. In most cases (the exceptions being a small minority of moorlands where shooting interests attempt to keep people off their heather moors with warning notices) it is possible to walk freely, as long as you have a good map and compass, strong footwear and sensible protective clothing.

Each of the valleys, or dales as they are usually known, has a different flavour and character. As you follow a stream down, it broadens, joining tributaries, to become a full-scale river, the high farms becoming hamlets or villages, and the villages mill or market towns. But always, just above the valley, there is the ever present moorland, somewhere to escape to, with that sense of wild space and freedom. Wherever you live, in towns like Huddersfield, Bradford, Halifax, and even Leeds, on a fine day you can see the moorland sweeping away to the west. You are aware of the open fell country so close to you, only a short car, bus or train journey away or, in many towns in Airedale, Wharfedale, Calderdale or the Colne Valley, only a short walk up a winding cobbled street or steep footpath.

Even where the valleys finally meander down to join the great plain of York east of Leeds or Wakefield, there is still a sense of the river valley, the dale in which you live that began its life in that western wilderness. Each dale creates a different kind of landscape within itself, and in West Yorkshire this means magnificent opportunities for walking. This need not be strenuous boots and rucksack stuff (though if you do not bring at least strong shoes on a visit to West Yorkshire you are missing a wonderful opportunity), as in many areas you can enjoy an easy stroll with much to do and see.

For convenience I have divided West Yorkshire's countryside into six main areas, each with a natural centre for its exploration.

Airedale and Brontë Country

The area of the Pennines between the Yorkshire Dales and the Peak District is known as the South Pennines and is becoming increasingly popular for outdoor holidays and recreation.

Its most famous single attraction is the old town of Haworth. The nearby Brontë Moors, in effect the moorlands which radiate away from the little river Worth, a tributary of the Aire, again offer superb walking. All lovers of the books and poems of the Brontë sisters will want to walk from Haworth's little cobbled main street to the Brontë Falls and on to Top Withins, reputedly the site of the 'Wuthering Heights' of the novel, perhaps going through Penistone Hill Country Park, an open area of moorland and waymarked paths, returning via the little village of Stanbury.

Part of the 250 mile (400 km) Pennine Way goes through Top Withins *en route* between Edale and Scotland. A very attractive walk from Haworth is to follow the Pennine Way south over to Calderdale or north to the green pastures of Craven and Lothersdale. There are also fine walks over to Calderdale through Hardcastle Crags over the Stair Dyke path from Oxenhope and routes over to Bingley in Airedale, itself an excellent centre for local riverside and canalside rambles. Haworth has a busy tourist information centre and Arthur Gemmell's excellent Haworth Footpath Map (Stile Maps), on sale at the centre, as well as the Ordnance Survey Outdoor Leisure Map of the South Pennines, will reveal countless opportunities to explore the Brontë Moors on foot.

Airedale and the northern fringes of Bradford, particularly around Shipley, Saltaire, Bingley, Baildon and Cullingworth, all offer fine walking. For a short morning or afternoon trip, walk (or take the Glen tramway) up Shipley Glen from Saltaire to Baildon Moor and the Bracken Hall Countryside Centre (Glen Road, Baildon, Bradford; telephone 0274 584140). Alternatively walk through Myrtle Park in Bingley to climb through the woods to St Ives Estate (to where the less energetic can take their cars direct), a magnificent, wooded area on the hillside above Airedale. Not far from St Ives, and reached by footpath, is Druids Altar, a gritstone outcrop and setting used by Disraeli for a meeting of the Chartists in his novel *Sybil*. It is still a magnificent natural feature and viewpoint.

Calderdale

Calderdale is the name of both a geographic region (the valley of the little river Calder, a very typical South Pennine river) and a local authority. Upper Calderdale (referring to the geography) is superb, a hidden jewel. The valley west of Halifax, which, curiously enough, is situated on a tributary valley, the Hebble, away from the main valley of the Calder, is steep-sided to an often breathtaking degree, a narrow chasm through the rugged hills, often bordered by steep gritstone crags. Not surprisingly, it is quite industrial, with a string of mill towns (Sowerby Bridge, Luddenden Foot, Mytholmroyd, Hebden Bridge, Todmorden) along the valley bottom. None of them, with the exception of Hebden Bridge, is particularly pretty, but they share that narrow space with a main road (the A646), railway

Beckfoot packhorse bridge crosses Harden Beck near Bingley.

and canal and countryside of great beauty, most particularly the side valleys, many of them thickly wooded with oak and birch woods as fine as any in England.

Hebden Bridge is the natural place to begin a visit to Upper Calderdale. It is a thriving little community which, in the 1980s, has undergone a dramatic change from a declining textile town to a tourist centre. The formerly derelict canal has reopened as a marina, hotels have followed and the tourist information centre has become a focal point of interest in the area.

The walking opportunities from Hebden Bridge are splendid. For a start, try the steep medieval cobbled way from the Tudor Hebden Bridge itself, which crosses Hebden Water and climbs by steps to the medieval weavers' settlement of Heptonstall, for all the world like a Mediterranean hill village except for the grey stone. Follow part of the Calderdale Way footpath above Colden Water. The Calderdale Way is a 50 mile (80 km) footpath route which follows attractive high-level paths and ways above Calderdale, with links into the valleys. (For details see the booklet published by the Calderdale Way Association and available from local bookshops and tourist information centres.)

Or, go by car or footpath to Hardcastle Crags, an almost Alpine-style, thickly wooded valley, a National Trust property whose oak-woods are a rich reserve of beauty and wildlife, including red squirrels, spotted wood-peckers and a particularly rare form of wood ant. You can park at the entrance to the Crags (to reach the car park take the signposted road which leaves the A6033 Hebden Bridge to Keighley road a mile, 1.5 km, north of Hebden Bridge) and a leaflet on sale at Hebden Bridge gives a choice of trails: both via Gibson Mill, a disused textile mill, to the Crags themselves, hidden deep in the woods, and along the neighbouring valley of Grimsworth Dean.

The more adventurous can explore the superb 'hidden' valley of Luddenden Dean, reached off the main A644 turning northwards on the signposted lane to Luddenden, Cragg Vale behind Mytholmroyd and the curious little moorland hamlets of Lumbutts and Mankinholes, where the great tower of Stoodley Pike (built to commemorate victory at Waterloo in 1815, then, after it had fallen down in 1854, rebuilt in 1856 to celebrate the Crimean War) dominates the moorland landscape. Lumbutts is signposted off the A6033 Todmorden to Rochdale road 2 miles (3 km) south of Todmorden. Walkers can also pick up the Pennine Way again from this point, leading down to Blackstone Edge and its ancient 'Roman' road.

Todmorden, a town very much at the crossroads between Lancashire and Yorkshire, offers fine walks through and above two remarkable natural passes of the Pennines: Summit Gap over to Littleborough, and Cliviger Gorge over to Burnley. Both passes are intertwined with ancient packhorse ways and paved causeways, as rich in interest for the transport historian as in attraction for the

Mills in the Colne Valley near Huddersfield.

casual rambler.

The Ryburn Valley, branching off Calderdale to form another side valley which climbs, past Ripponden and a series of reservoirs, to the moorland summit of Blackstone Edge, is another fine area to explore, with interesting walks around the reservoirs.

In the central part of Calderdale there is an extremely attractive area of semi-natural countryside around West Vale, Greetland (just off the Elland road from Halifax at SE 097214), at Clay House and North Dean Information Centre, the start of the Calderdale Way and a fascinating nature trail through North Dean Woods.

However, one of the most impressive areas of South Pennines countryside in Calderdale is man-made: Scammonden Reservoir, a huge expanse of water held back by a great dam that now carries the M62, arguably Britain's most spectacular stretch of motorway, over the summit of the Pennines. The area around the reservoir is now an informal country park, with good footpath access and places from which to look at the many dinghies sailing on the water. It is best reached from the Kirklees side, turning off the A640 Huddersfield to Rochdale road before reaching Nont Sarahs pub along signposted lanes to car parks close to the reservoir edge, but footpaths from Ripponden can be followed which lead under the M62 motorway.

The Colne Valley and the Peak District

The Colne Valley west of Huddersfield is, like Upper Calderdale, dominated by river, road, railway and canal running along a narrow valley bottom but it is of a quite different character, being more open and less steep-sided, though with its own special attraction. Marsden, at the head of the valley, is its natural focal point, a mill town in a great green bowl of hills from which there are several ways west: either through Standedge by canal or rail tunnel, or over the top by Standedge Pass, or by the ancient packhorse way known as Rapes Highway, another superb walk.

Tunnel End Canal and Countryside Centre (Reddisher Road, Marsden; telephone 0484 846062) has a choice of leaflets and walks, including the Standedge Trail, a series of routes following old paths and tracks. The most unusual of these is surely the early nineteenth-century 'Boat Lane' followed by canal horses when barges were being 'legged' through the tunnel (see chapter 9). You can reach the centre by following signs from Marsden village past the railway station, crossing the railway and turning left down to the Junction Inn.

Another way out of Marsden is southwards into the Peak District National Park, soon reached through the Wessenden Valley, where a series of superb reservoirs dominates an otherwise grandly empty landscape.

Reservoirs fringe the Peak District at the Holme Valley side too, with, above the little village of Holme, a combination of high moorland, forest and reservoir more reminiscent of the Scottish Highlands than the Pennines. This beautiful area, which again has a rich choice of walks from Holme or the popular town of Holmfirth, is the least known and perhaps least visited part of the Peak District National Park, cut off as it is from the rest of the Peak by the great moorland ridge of Holme Moss, the pass across which rises nearly 1718 feet (524 metres) above sea level and is still a formidable obstacle for drivers in the winter months.

Local footpath maps of the Colne Valley and Holme valleys (produced by the Colne Valley and Meltham civic societies respectively) are on sale at Tunnel End Centre and Holmfirth tourist information centre.

Leeds and the east

Of all Britain's major cities, Leeds can boast that it is the greenest, having more parks per head of the population than any other city in Europe, as well as claiming Europe's largest urban park, at Temple Newsam. It is not just the parks which make Leeds such an attractive city, but its long, narrow strips of semi-natural woodland, such as those which now form the Meanwood Valley Trail through Woodhouse, Meanwood and Adel.

Perhaps because of topography, the evolution of Leeds on the Pennine foothills, as a scattered conglomeration of villages rather than a single major settlement, makes it possible to walk from almost the city centre through woods and fields. The northern fringes of the city in particular are unusually pleasant areas like Headingley, Cookridge, Roundhay, Alwoodley and Shadwell and still keep much of their rural character. You can walk through uninterrupted countryside from Roundhay Park to Wetherby or Harewood and Otley, from Cookridge through Chevin Forest Park (an area of magnificent woodland on the ridge above Otley) to Ilkley or Harrogate, or from Seacroft to Knaresborough or York.

The White House Information Centre (Chevin Forest Park, Otley, Leeds; telephone 0943 462454) has small interpretative displays of local wildlife and can be reached by signed footpath from Otley town centre.

Though there are pleasant fringes to the south (Middleton Woods) and the west (Tong-Cockersdale Country Park, which is shared with Bradford), it is the countryside to the east that will surprise the visitor: the old market town of Wetherby on the A1, the Georgian resort of Boston Spa, the coaching town of Aberford, Ledsham with its Saxon church. Much of this special and unsuspected charm is caused by a happy accident of geology: a belt of Magnesian limestone, a soft creamy-coloured stone, which not only provides a magnificent building material for cottage, bridge or church (the most famous building from the stone is York Minster) but gives a gentler, softer feel to the landscape and a richly fertile soil. The landscape around Wetherby, Clifford and Boston Spa, indeed right down to Wentbridge, south of Wakefield, has been described as a miniature Cotswolds, an undulating countryside of old farms and villages, most with ancient churches, and of scattered copses, little streams and mature parkland.

A visitor to Leeds is also recommended to take the Meanwood Valley Trail out to Golden Acre Park, with its superb mixture of semi-natural woodland park, lake and botanic garden, or the Leeds Country Way, a 60 mile (97 km) route that circumnavigates the city by footpath. In addition, a useful set of leaflets tells you how to explore West Yorkshire's limestone country; all are available from bookshops in the city or from the Leeds tourist information centre in Wellington Street.

Wakefield's countryside

Wakefield may not normally receive recognition for its countryside, dominated as much of the area is by coal mining, but, south of the city, sometimes close to the actual coal workings, a beautiful area of scattered woodland and parkland extends towards the South Yorkshire boundary, of quite different character to the Pennines, and provides delightful areas for quiet exploration. Most notable is Bretton Park, the great estate which contains the College of Education and the Yorkshire Sculpture Park. There are delightful walks around the park and nature reserves as well as footpath links between Bretton and nearby Cannon Park in South Yorkshire.

Further eastwards, the lakes of Newmillerdam (on the A61 4 miles, 6 km, south of Wakefield) provide a notable bird sanctuary, with, among other fine species, Canada geese and great crested grebe, whilst paths link Haw Park and Wintersett Reservoir with Nostell Priory, its park and gardens, only a short distance away.

Bird lovers will enjoy Fairburn Ings, near Castleford, reached off the A656 Aberford/Garforth-Castleford road, where large parking bays enable even the most amateur ornithologists to enjoy spectacular sightings of geese, swans and waders on otherwise uninspiring pit 'flashes' on the edge of the great Yorkshire coalfields. This 600 acre (240 ha) reserve includes an extensive wetland habitat and is maintained by the Royal Society for the Protection of Birds.

This is more Midland than Northern countryside, rich rolling farmland and scattered woods rather than moorland and valley, different in feeling and flavour, and particularly lovely towards the villages of Ackworth, Badsworth and Wentbridge, where the Magnesian limestone belt adds its distinctive colour to walls, churches and fertile soils.

Wharfedale

The Yorkshire Dales National Park ends within a few hundred metres of the West Yorkshire boundary, but the characteristic and world-famous scenery most certainly does not, and the area of mid Wharfedale, which includes Addingham, Otley and above all Ilkley, provides splendid walking opportunities. You can follow the river Wharfe itself from Ilkley's old bridge to Addingham and Bolton Abbey, continuing, if you have the time and inclination, for a full 81 miles (130 km) to the Lake District, a route which forms the Dales Way, one of the most dramatically beautiful walks in England. Or, if you want to walk in another situation, through scenery perhaps not as dramatic but full of character and charm, the 71 mile (114 km) Ebor Way will take you via Otley, Chevin, Harewood, Boston Spa and Tadcaster to York.

Ilkley is the natural focal point of mid Wharfedale, and the renowned Ilkley Moor of the song ('Ilkley Moor Baht 'At') lies immediately to the south of the town, dominating its little main thoroughfare, Brook Street, like a great upreared Alpine slope. Ilkley Moor is truly impressive, whether you are a casual stroller or a serious hiker. An ancient urban common (upon which the public have unlimited rights to roam), it offers miles of meandering paths, through bracken, heather and bilberry, and superb views across the dale. Strictly speaking, Ilkley Moor consists only of that part of the great watershed between Wharfedale and Airedale within Ilkley town itself. 'Greater Ilkley Moor', consisting of Addingham High Moor and Burley Moor as well as the moorlands on the Airedale side, forms part of Rombalds Moor, named after a legendary giant. One of the great classic walks of the area is to follow the paved way from the eighteenth-century bath house at White Wells across Rombalds Moor to Bingley in Airedale. Another favourite is to follow a choice of paths around the edge of the Moor to the Swastika Stone and Windgate Nick above Addingham and on to Silsden and Keighley.

You will find all these and many more routes in the Ilkley Moor Footpath Map, produced by the West Riding Ramblers Association and on sale in local shops and at the excellent little tourist information centre in the library (almost opposite the railway station).

The Cow and Calf Rocks on Ilkley Moor.

Shipley Glen Rocks on Baildon Moor.

3
Archaeological sites

West Yorkshire is particularly rich in archaeological sites, especially in the upland areas. However, the casual visitor will not necessarily find much to see on the ground: interpretation of the sites is limited and it is often useful to visit a local museum to discover more about the finds from a particular area.

What follows is a small selection of the most accessible sites in the county.

NEOLITHIC

Castle Hill, Almondbury (SE 153141).

Castle Hill is one of the most important archaeological sites in West Yorkshire. Excavations have proved that this 900 foot (275 metre) high ridge, commanding impressive views down the Colne and Holme valleys and with a natural defence on three sides, was first occupied by neolithic settlers around 2000 BC. These were herdsmen from Europe with the ability to make simple tools, who built a simple earthen bank and ditch to defend their homestead.

From 600 BC iron age settlers developed Castle Hill as a fortress, but a disastrous fire a hundred years later destroyed it and the site remained deserted for the next 1600 years until, in AD 1147, the Normans restored the earthworks by creating a motte and bailey castle. The castle continued in use for Norman hunting parties and a well was dug through the solid rock in the fourteenth century. The site became a beacon and was used for various public events over the ensuing centuries.

A tavern was built in 1812 and replaced in 1852 by the present public house, whilst the Jubilee Tower was erected in 1899 to commemorate Queen Victoria's Diamond Jubilee.

Many of the excavated finds from Castle Hill are kept in the Tolson Museum, Huddersfield (see chapter 7).

Ringstone Edge, Ripponden (SE 045183).

This site consists of a stone circle and cairn which formed part of a neolithic settlement on Ringstone Edge Moor.

BRONZE AGE

Ilkley Moor

Ilkley Moor is an area rich in bronze age remains: circles, standing stones and mysterious 'cup and ring' stones. These last are outcropping boulders with complex markings, the origins of which are obscure; they might be some form of boundary stone, perhaps delineating sacred territory. There are several good examples on the moorland slopes between Cow and Calf Rocks (SE 130468) and Silver Well Cottage (SE 104467), though you will need a large-scale map and a pair of rambling boots to locate them. A particularly fine example is just below the moor-edge path (itself probably of bronze age origin) on Addingham High Moor (SE 085472).

A very fine stone circle, known as the Twelve Apostles, is passed on the Ilkley to Dick Hudson's footpath at SE 126451. Not all the stones remain standing. Most famous of all, however, is the mysterious Swastika Stone, a late bronze age 'follyfoot' or symbol of eternity carved on a flat rock, protected by a fence on the moor-edge footpath just above Heber's Ghyll (SE 097469), an impressive monument and a fine viewpoint.

Those not wishing to climb so far can see a fine 'cup and ring' stone in the gardens opposite St Margaret's churchyard, Queen's Road, Ilkley (SE 115473), whilst the Manor House Museum (see chapter 7) has a number of interesting publications about the stones and their history.

Baildon Moor (SE 138403).

This is another important area for 'cup and ring' stones. There is a stone circle, known as the Soldier's Trench, on Baildon Green close to Bracken Hall Countryside Centre (see chapter 2).

Hawksworth Moor (SE 134435).

In the centre of the moor, not far from Horncliffe Well House, there is an oval of stones, the widest being some 43 feet (13 metres) across. 46 of the stones can be seen set together. Part of the inner circle was probably a burial chamber.

IRON AGE

Aberford

Two great ridged embankments, known as Becca Banks (SE 423382) and The Rein (SE 440377), cut across the Great North Road (A1) and may have been the lines of a Brigantian defensive fortification built to prevent the invading Roman army moving northwards.

Ilkley (SE 130360).

There are iron age settlement remains near Green Crag Slack, including a possible village settlement which is still being investigated.

ROMAN

Castleford

Undoubtedly the most important Roman site in West Yorkshire is at Castleford: a fort, *Lagentium*, on the Great North Road, long since lost under industrialisation. Many archaeological finds have, however, been recovered and are displayed either at the small specialist Roman museum in Castleford Library or in the Wakefield Museum (see chapter 7).

Ilkley

The foundations of the Roman fort at Ilkley (*Olicana*), which guarded the original ford over the river Wharfe, are still visible immediately to the east of the parish church (SE 117478). There are several Roman altars in the Manor House Museum (see chapter 7), whilst another is to be found in the woods at Middleton Lodge (SE 109492).

Roman roads

The Roman road from Skipton to Boroughbridge can still be traced below Addingham High Moor through Street Farm (SE 078490). The name 'street' denotes an old paved road or green way.

A more controversial Roman road crosses the Lancashire-Yorkshire boundary at Blackstone Edge. Some scholars argue that the superb stretch of paved causeway on the Lancashire side (SE 974172) is medieval, rather than Roman, linking to the packhorse way down the Ryburn Valley, whilst others claim documentary proof of Roman origins.

MEDIEVAL

Eastergate Bridge. Reached by footpath from New Hey Lane end (SE 029122).

A packhorse bridge, probably medieval in origin although rebuilt in the eighteenth century, lies on the ancient packhorse way, Rapes Highway, which leads from Littleborough and Rochdale to Marsden.

East Riddlesden Barn (SE 079422). On the A629 near Keighley.

A medieval tithe barn lies in the grounds of East Riddlesden Hall (see chapter 6). Of enormous dimensions, it is one of the finest in the north of England, probably originally built by the monks of Bolton Priory. The monastic fish pond also survives.

Ilkley

The ancient spring at White Wells, around which in the eighteenth century Squire Myddleton built his bath house (the origin of Ilkley as a spa town), can be visited by moorland path from the road to Ilkley Moor (SE 118476). There are three outstanding Anglo-Saxon crosses in the church (see chapter 5).

Mount Cross (SD 914272).

The shaft of a medieval stone cross marks the line of the Long Causeway, an ancient trade route above Todmorden from the Calder Valley through Cliviger Gorge. Part of this

Rocks with 'cup and ring' marks, near St Margaret's churchyard, Ilkley.

route can still be followed, though much of its length is a tarmac road.

Te Deum Stone (SD 570231).

A medieval waymarking stone is found on the Calderdale Way (see chapter 2) above Todmorden, on the summit of the packhorse way between Cragg and Mankinholes. This is where, according to tradition, coffins were rested when corpses were being carried to consecrated ground. The Latin inscription of *'Te deum laudamus'* means 'We praise thee, O Lord'.

Sandal Castle, a Norman motte and bailey.

4
Castles and monastic ruins

Harewood Castle. Visible from the main A61 Leeds to Harrogate road, but no public access.

This is an impressively sited fourteenth-century ruin overlooking the Wharfe valley from Harewood Park.

Kirkstall Abbey, Leeds. Situated on the A65 Leeds-Ilkley trunk road, about 3 miles (5 km) from the city centre.

Kirkstall Abbey is acknowledged to be the finest complete example of an early Cistercian abbey in Britain. Constructed between 1152 and 1182 by Abbot Alexander, most of the original fabric survives with only minor alterations from the fifteenth and sixteenth centuries. It is constructed from millstone grit quarried locally at Bramley Falls by the river Aire.

The abbey is built to a typical Cistercian plan, not dissimilar to Fountains Abbey in North Yorkshire: as the monks who founded it came from Fountains this is not coincidental. Particularly noteworthy are the nave with massive Norman arches, some excellent, though simple, decoration and the well preserved outbuildings, including a thirteenth-century infirmary, refectory, malthouse and gatehouse.

Unusually for a Cistercian ruin of this date, most of the buildings still stand to their original height, despite their absorption into industrial and inner suburban Leeds and their use, after the Dissolution in 1539, as a local source of building stone. The picturesque ruins inspired many painters, including Cotman, Girtin and Turner, as well as the poet Thomas Gray. No doubt it was the interest of these artists that saved the ruins from further destruction though, during the industrial revolution and afterwards, they became encrusted with soot-black grime.

The ruins now stand in a pleasant area of parkland, while the gatehouse, on the opposite side of the main road, now forms part of the Abbey House Museum (see chapter 7).

Pontefract Castle, Pontefract. Reached on foot from the town centre.

Built by Ilbert de Lacy in the eleventh century, this castle, whose remains still dominate the ancient town of Pontefract, was once one of the most formidable fortresses in Britain. The castle later passed to the house of Lancaster and became a royal castle when Henry Bolingbroke was made Henry IV in

1399. This castle, Shakespeare's Pomfret, was the scene of the death of Richard II.

It was a major royalist stronghold in the Civil War; it is possible to visit the underground chamber where prisoners were kept and carved their names into the rock. The castle was demolished after the Civil War and now only the lower part of the keep and the line of the inner bailey wall can be seen.

The oldest parts of the castle to survive are the foundations of St Clement's Chapel and part of the twelfth-century bailey wall with a postern gateway. The keep, or Round Tower, dates from the thirteenth century; its foundations are dug out of solid rock.

Sandal Castle, near Wakefield (SE 337182). Reached off the A61 2 miles (3 km) south of Wakefield.

A typical example of a Norman motte and bailey castle, this was the stronghold of the manor of Wakefield, which covered large tracts of the Calder Valley.

At times Sandal Castle played a part in national history: the battle of Wakefield in 1460 (as mentioned in Shakespeare's play *Henry VI Part 3*), which ended in the death of the Duke of York, was fought beneath the castle walls. The castle was garrisoned for the King during the Civil War and, after a siege, was demolished on the orders of Parliament. Little more remains than the foundation walls, but many of the objects found during extensive archaeological excavations can be seen at Wakefield Museum (see chapter 7).

The ruins of Kirkstall Abbey, near Leeds.

5
Churches

What West Yorkshire lacks in monastic remains, it amply compensates for in churches of almost every period and style. Its ancient parish churches are among the finest in the land: two have become cathedrals in their own right.

Addingham: St Peter.
This is a handsome church in a fine setting close to the river Wharfe. It overlooks an extensive green with a small stone footbridge over the beck leading to the church. Though it mostly dates from the mid eighteenth century, the church is Perpendicular in origin, built in the latter half of the fifteenth century. A late Anglo-Saxon cross in the church indicates, however, that this building is on the site of a far older church; this is perhaps linked with the fact that in AD 970 Archbishop Wulfere of York is reputed to have fled to Addingham to hide from the Danes.

Adel: St John the Baptist.
Adel's church dates from the twelfth century and is one of the best and most complete Norman churches in the north of England. It has a nave and chancel but no tower or apse. The nave is wide, with very small windows in the east and west, and corbel friezes (blocks of stone projecting from the window) with human faces and beasts along the side; there is a similar frieze along the western gable. There is a famous arched doorway full of intricate carving which owes much to Anglo-Saxon tradition, though dating from around 1150. The doorway columns are badly preserved, but there are capitals with intertwined hands and leaves, animals, zigzags and rolls, a rare Norman door ring showing a monster swallowing a man, and much exciting carving besides.

Bradford Cathedral.

Bardsey: All Hallows.
This small country church has a rare Anglo-Saxon tower, though the top of the tower and the rest of the church are Perpendicular or later. Earlier Norman aisles (probably built into the original Saxon church) survive.

Bradford: Cathedral Church of St Peter.
A cathedral only since 1919, this fine building dates from the fourteenth century, though with considerable enlargement in Victorian times. It is constructed, fittingly enough, of millstone grit. Occupying a site where a church has existed since the seventh century, its west tower, in the Perpendicular style, rises magnificently above the city centre. In spite of changes, the interior remains predominantly medieval, with decorated arches and piers. The font has a wonderful late Gothic cover, with a tall spire and a filigree of carved buttresses and tracery. There is also some Anglo-Saxon sculpture and stained glass windows made by William Morris's workshop in 1862, reputed to contain the work of Ford Madox Brown, Rossetti and Burne-Jones.

One of the most fascinating memorials is that to Joseph Priestley, one of the engineers of the Leeds and Liverpool Canal, which served Bradford; his memorial shows a relief model of the canal building in progress.

During the Civil War the parish church (as it was then) withstood Royalists guns (Bradford was a Parliamentary stronghold) by using woolsacks to absorb the impact of cannonballs.

Bramhope: Puritan Chapel.
This is a simple, austere building which was erected in Oliver Cromwell's time (1649) on the ancient highway up Pool Bank. It consists of a plain, oblong structure with straight, mullioned windows. The three-decker pulpit contains two original pewboxes arranged to focus the listeners' attention on the pulpit. The hexagonal font is dated 1673.

Clifford: St Edward (Roman Catholic).

This is one of the most impressive Victorian churches in Yorkshire. It was built in 1845-8 to the design of a young Scottish architect named Ramsey, with a tower added in 1859-60. Money for the building of the church was subscribed by the Pope, the Queen of France, the King of Sardinia and the Grand Duke of Parma, as well as a local family, the Grimsons, who owned a flax mill in Clifford.

The style of the church is Romanesque, with a tall western porch under the tower, and strong, circular piers in the nave decorated in a similar style to those in Durham Cathedral.

The statue of the Virgin was executed by Hoffman, a Jewish sculptor from Rome who was so moved by his own work that he changed his faith while completing it. Four of the stained glass windows are said to have been designed by Pugin.

Dewsbury: All Saints.

Dewsbury was once the centre of an enormous parish which extended high into the Pennines as far as the Lancashire border. The parish church dates from the twelfth century, with a good deal of thirteenth-century work. There are fragments of an important Anglo-Saxon cross and coffin lids of the same period. The tower was designed by the celebrated Yorkshire architect John Carr in 1767, with further restoration taking place in the 1880s.

The church is well known for the tradition of tolling the Devil's Knell on Christmas Eve with a bell evocatively known as 'Black Tom'.

Halifax: St John.

This is one of the largest parish churches in England, of almost cathedral-like proportions, reflecting the great size and wealth of this parish in earlier times. Much of the building dates back to the twelfth and thirteenth centuries, though most, including the great western tower, was built in the fifteenth century.

The fine wooden ceilings in the nave and chancel date from 1635, whilst the unusually austere windows are from Commonwealth times. There are also a superb communion rail, richly decorated, a magnificent fifteenth-century spired font cover, some unusual poppy-head decoration on the stalls and handsome Georgian memorials.

One of the most memorable items in the church is Old Tristram, a remarkable life-sized wooden painted effigy of a beggar, reputedly based on a local character and for many years the church poor box, collecting alms for the needy.

Holmfirth: Holy Trinity.

A large, handsome eighteenth-century church in the town centre, this was built in

One of the Anglo-Saxon crosses in Ilkley church.

1777-87 in neo-classical style to the designs of Joseph Jaggar and is very much a town church. The gable faces the street and the tower is constructed at the eastern end, against a steep hillside: space was always at a premium in the Holme Valley. The building has two storeys, with round-headed lower windows and segmented-headed upper windows, and three galleries inside.

Ilkley: All Saints.

This typical Dales church, dating back to the thirteenth century, has a short Perpendicular tower and a low, clerestoried nave of the sixteenth century, though much, including the chancel, was heavily restored in Victorian times. There is a fine Jacobean font cover and a tiny medieval doorway at the back of the church.

The glory of Ilkley church is, however, three magnificent Anglian crosses, one with its original head and dating from the ninth century. Formerly standing in the churchyard, they have been moved into the church and are beautifully displayed under the tower. Their wealth of intricate carving (of beasts, vine scrolls, angels and Christ) makes them one of the finest examples of Anglo-Saxon carving in the North.

Ledsham: All Saints.

This is a superb Anglo-Saxon church, one of the finest in Yorkshire. It dates probably from the eighth century and, as you stand in the little building, you can trace the outline of the original tiny church and see where it was enlarged in later centuries (including the tower, which was heightened from a Saxon base in Norman times). Some Victorian restoration has taken place but is in keeping with the original. There is some fine surviving Anglo-Saxon carving and impressive seventeenth- and eighteenth-century memorials, in particular a marble carving of Lady Betty Hastings, a notable intellectual and bluestocking who founded a nearby orphanage.

Leeds: St John, Briggate.

St John's church in New Briggate is of special interest because it is one of the very few churches built in England during the seventeenth century. It is architecturally particularly fine. Externally, the church looks typically Perpendicular, with a fine western tower, aisle, chancel, porch (all embattled) and some elaborate tracery. Internally, the roof has tie beams, kingposts and corbels representing angels and musicians. Another remarkable feature is that the church has two naves of the same width and length.

There is a memorial in the nave to John Harrison, the wealthy Leeds cloth merchant whose generosity allowed the church to be built as a gift to the newly incorporated borough of Leeds, a town rapidly growing in size and importance owing to the increasingly prosperous clothing trade.

The church was restored in 1868 with great sensitivity by the leading Victorian architect Norman Shaw and remains one of Leeds's most impressive buildings.

Leeds: Holy Trinity, Boar Lane.

This superb Georgian church was designed by a Mr Halfpeny in 1727, though in 1839 its tower had to be replaced with an unusual square spire, after it had been destroyed in a gale. The church is notable for its magnificent interior, with giant Corinthian columns supporting an elegant tunnel vault, and richly carved pews which were installed in 1886.

Leeds: St Peter.

Leeds's original medieval parish church was replaced between 1838 and 1841 in a mixture of styles which nevertheless have a unity. Galleries, heavily decorated with canopies, extend along the nave. There are some fine monuments and an especially impressive Anglo-Saxon cross, as well as memorials and effigies from the earlier church.

The building of the railway through the centre of Leeds in the 1840s severed the church from the city centre; many gravestones were used to pave the railway embankment.

Leeds: St Anne's (Roman Catholic) cathedral.

Like Liverpool, Leeds has a twentieth-century cathedral, built between 1902 and 1904 to the designs of J. H. Eastwood in the 'Arts and Crafts' Gothic style. The reredos in the south chancel chapel is by Nicholas Pugin.

Meltham: St Bartholomew.

Of the original 1651 church, only the date stone above the porch survives with a date tablet on the pulpit and some mullioned windows with round-headed lights which were re-used, with characteristic Yorkshire thrift, in a cottage opposite the church. Most of the church is of the late eighteenth century with Victorian additions, including the tower, which has Tuscan pilasters and urn pinnacles.

Otley: All Saints.

This is a handsome church reflecting the wealth and importance of this market town from medieval times. Norman windows and a doorway survive, as do many fragments of Anglo-Saxon crosses and part of a late Viking grave slab. Much of the church is Decorated or Perpendicular in style, with later additions and some fine monuments.

There is a moving monument in the churchyard to the men who died in 1845-9 building the nearby Bramhope railway tunnel on the Leeds to Harrogate line. It is in the form of a scale model of the crenellated tunnel entrance.

Pontefract: All Saints.

Built in the magnificent ruins of the great medieval church below the castle (destroyed in Cromwell's bombardment), the present church dates from 1830 and incorporates part of the older church's stonework and tracery.

Pontefract: St Giles.

St Giles's, a fine, mainly eighteenth-century church near Pontefract's Buttermarket, became the parish church in 1789. It has a large, octagonal storey on the tower and fine flying buttresses.

Wakefield: Cathedral Church of All Saints.

The soaring spire of Wakefield Cathedral, at 247 feet (75 metres) the highest in West Yorkshire and a landmark for miles around, was first erected in 1420 but was rebuilt from 1858 to 1874 by Sir George Gilbert Scott. Though heavily restored, the essential medieval quality of the building remains as a central feature of the town.

Wakefield Cathedral began life as a parish church, becoming a cathedral only in 1888. Its origins lie in the twelfth century, with much fifteenth-century work. The font dates from 1661 and there are some fine carvings: for example, misericords, including a juggler with his head between his legs, a Tudor rose and a pelican. There is a handsome eighteenth-century three-decker pulpit.

Wakefield: St John, Wood Street.

A beautiful Regency church, this is in a fine square of the same period, a relic of Wakefield's gracious past and former importance as a 'county' town. The church, decorated in neo-classical style, has an elegant western tower and a Tuscan doorway.

Wakefield: Bridge Chapel (St Mary's).

This is a medieval chapel on a bridge, only four examples of which remain in England: at Rotherham, St Ives (Cambridgeshire), Bradford-on-Avon and Wakefield. The one at Wakefield is reputed to be the finest. Built in 1350 on Chantry Bridge, the chapel served two purposes: to collect money for the upkeep of the bridge and, as a shrine, to protect travellers from danger when crossing a ford.

The small shrine is built in Decorated style around a facade of five bays with three small doorways, all with elaborate tracery. On the parapet there are fine reliefs of the Pentecost and a spiral staircase into the turret. The building was, however, heavily restored in 1847, and again in 1939.

Whitkirk: St Mary.

This fine medieval church, in fourteenth-century Perpendicular style, is on the outskirts of Leeds.

Among the memorials are a moving monument to the young Viscount Irwin of nearby Temple Newsam, his wife and their only daughter, who died at the age of two, and also the grave of John Smeaton (1724-94), the great eighteenth-century Leeds engineer, who was born in Whitkirk and who built the third Eddystone Lighthouse (portrayed on his tomb).

The Bridge Chapel at Wakefield.

Bolling Hall, Bradford, a medieval house with later extensions and alterations.

6
Historic houses and gardens

There are a number of outstanding country houses and gardens in West Yorkshire which are open to the public, including several of national importance. For details of opening times and charges for admission enquire directly.

Bolling Hall, Bowling Hall Road, Bradford BD4 7LP. Telephone: 0274 723057. 2 miles (3 km) south of the city centre.

A fine medieval house, Bolling Hall has been extended over the centuries to give a fascinating mixture of styles, including extensive Tudor and eighteenth-century wings.

Now a Bradford city museum, the house contains fine Tudor and Jacobean furniture, an elegant eighteenth-century bedroom in the Chinese style (with green and cream matching furniture originally made for the famous actor David Garrick) and a red damask room with a Chippendale bed designed for Harewood House. Also of interest is a window (about 1500) containing the coats of arms of leading Yorkshire families. There are collections of seventeenth-century oak furniture, domestic utensils and toys.

One of the most moving exhibits is the room devoted to the memory of the Bradford Regiment (the 'Bradford Pals'), which was almost totally wiped out in the battle of the Somme in the First World War. The house is reputed to have a ghost, linked with events of the Civil War and the siege of Bradford.

Bolling Park, opposite the hall, is an attractive town park, with flower beds and small conservatories, offering fine views across the central area of Bradford.

Bramham Park, near Wetherby LS23 6ND. Telephone: 0937 844265. Signposted from Bramham village just off A1.

Bramham Park is an impressive Queen Anne house, built between 1698 and 1710 for Robert Benson, Lord Bingley, a former Lord Mayor of York who became Lord Chamberlain to Queen Anne. Superbly proportioned in an elegant classical style, the effect is more French than English. The house has fine furniture and porcelain, and an impressive collection of paintings, including portraits by Kneller and Sir Joshua Reynolds.

Of special importance at Bramham are the gardens. They are amongst the finest examples in England of formal gardens and parkland in the manner of Louis XIV at Versailles: superb ornamental ponds and canals, cascades, statues, formal beech hedges, temples, summerhouses and obelisks, long avenues and vistas, creating a remarkable and harmonious landscape unity with the house. The grounds have many splendid mature trees, including cedars, copper beeches, Spanish chestnuts and wild rhododendrons.

Clay House, West Vale, Greetland, Halifax (SE 097214).

This impressive seventeenth-century yeoman's house, with its high gables and mullioned windows, was the home of the Clay family of West Vale. It has an unusual aisled barn. A Roman altar, dated to AD 208, was found locally and is now in the Fitzwilliam Museum, Cambridge. A replica is kept at Clay House.

Clay House now forms part of the North Dean Countryside Centre (see chapter 2).

East Riddlesden Hall, Bradford Road, Keighley BD20 5EL. Telephone: 0535 607075. National Trust. On A650 2 miles (3 km) east of Keighley.

This fascinating house dates back to a 'banqueting hall' built in 1602, though the main part was erected in 1648 for James Murgatroyd, a Halifax clothier and merchant. It is a house of dark stone gables and mullioned windows, and with many special features, including the original central hall, superb period fireplaces, oak panelling, decorated plaster ceilings and a magnificent rose window. Sadly, the west wing, added in 1692 to give the building symmetry, was demolished some years ago, but its facade remains.

East Riddlesden Hall is now furnished in period style. There are carefully restored Jacobean gardens to the rear of the house. In the monastic tithe barn (see chapter 3) there is a collection of farm wagons, machinery and implements.

Farnley Park, Old Farnley, Leeds. Reached off A58 Leeds to Halifax road 1 mile (1.5 km) west of Leeds ring road, turning northwards at New Farnley village.

Although Farnley Hall, a fine Georgian house, is not open to the public, its gardens, partially walled, and parkland are, making an attractive area to stroll in.

Harewood House, Harewood, Leeds LS17 9LQ. Telephone: 0532 886265. On A61, the main Leeds to Harrogate road.

One of the finest houses in the region and the home of the Earl of Harewood, cousin of Her Majesty the Queen, Harewood House was built in magnificent classical style, with massive Corinthian columns, by John Carr of York in 1759. Its southern facade was remodelled by Sir Charles Barry in 1843.

The interiors of the house were executed by Robert Adam in 1765 and constitute one of its main glories. The richly ornamental plasterwork was decorated by such artists as Angelica Kaufmann and Zucchi. There are many examples of furniture by Chippendale and other great craftsmen. The paintings include old masters and those by Reynolds, Gainsborough and others, and there is a superb collection of

Harewood House, home of the Earl of Harewood.

The Gothic Menagerie House at Nostell Priory.

Chinese and Sèvres porcelain.

Harewood Park was originally landscaped by 'Capability' Brown, with extensive parkland, artificial lakes, bridges and terraces. There are extensive rose gardens, woodland walks and a bird garden and butterfly house.

Holden Park, Oakworth, Keighley. On B6143 Keighley to Oakworth road.

A small but unusual little park, with a series of elaborate stone grottoes around a central bowling green and stone *arc de triomphe,* this is an elaborate and extraordinary folly.

Lotherton Hall, Aberford, Leeds LS25 3EB. Telephone: 0532 813259. 1½ miles (2.5 km) from Aberford village, just off A1.

This is a delightful Edwardian country house in a rural estate. The house was owned by Sir Avary Gascoigne, British ambassador to Russia and Japan, and was presented to the City of Leeds in 1968. (Sir Avary and Lady Gascoigne lost their only son in the invasion of Europe in 1944.) Lotherton now houses part of Leeds's extensive collections of paintings, furniture (especially *art nouveau* and 1930s) and ceramics (including a major Chinese collection) and a constantly changing costume gallery.

The grounds contain small but beautiful formal gardens, including Japanese, Italian and Alpine gardens, and a chapel which dates from Norman times. There are also woodland walks and trails and a large and interesting bird garden with a wide variety of species.

Meanwood Park and **The Hollies,** Leeds. Reached from Meanwood Road or Weetwood Lane.

This is a superb semi-natural woodland and parkland area formed from the gardens of two Victorian country houses. The Hollies has an outstanding Victorian formal garden with magnolias, rhododendrons and azaleas. Meanwood Park forms part of the Meanwood Valley Trail (see chapter 2).

Nostell Priory, Doncaster Road, Nostell, near Wakefield WF4 1QE. Telephone: 0942 863892. National Trust. On A638 Wakefield to Doncaster road.

Nostell Priory is a large Palladian-style house on the site of an Augustinian priory, built to the design of James Paine between 1733 and 1750 and generally acknowledged to be his masterpiece (though Paine's designs were never fully completed). Robert Adam added a northern wing in the 1770s. It is the ancestral and family home of Lord St Oswald.

The interior matches the outside design in the elegance of its decoration, mainly by Adam, who was then at the height of his powers, with ceiling paintings by Zucchi among others, as well as canvases by Van Dyck and Hogarth. Outstanding at Nostell is the collection of Chippendale furniture, held to be the finest in Britain, which was made to order for the house. One item which always attracts visitors' attention is a dolls' house, made about 1735 for the children of the fourth

Baronet, a replica of a grand country house with its original furnishings (according to tradition made by the young Thomas Chippendale himself).

There are extensive grounds, including rose gardens, parkland, ornamental lakes and woodland walks, and, near the park entrance, the medieval Wragby church, in Perpendicular style, noted for its outstanding collection of Swiss glass.

Oakwell Hall and Country Park, Nutter Lane, Birstall, near Batley. Telephone: 0924 474926. Signposted lane off A652 Dewsbury to Bradford road, or off B6126 Drighlington to Birstall road.

Oakwell Hall was built in stone in 1583 on the site of an earlier timber manor house and has remained little altered since, being one of the finest examples of its type in England. There is some fine decorated oak panelling, as well as oak floors, mullioned windows, ornate plaster ceilings and a splendid gallery. The hall is furnished with seventeenth-century oak furniture and domestic utensils. It also has strong literary associations, being the original 'Fieldhead' in Charlotte Bronte's novel *Shirley*.

The formal gardens at Oakwell Hall are laid out in seventeenth-century style with a period wall and raised terrace. An arboretum of exotic species and a wildlife garden are sited close by.

87 acres (35.2 ha) of the original Oakwell estate are now open as a country park, with nature trails, bridleways, an adventure playground and an equestrian arena. A visitor complex demonstrates crafts.

Red House, Oxford Road, Gomersal, Cleckheaton BD19 4JP. Telephone: 0274 872165.

Red House is a seventeenth-century house unusually (for West Yorkshire) built in brick. It was considerably remodelled in the early nineteenth century and is now furnished as a period house of around 1820. Red House was lived in continuously by the Taylor family of Gomersal from 1666 until the 1920s. Mary Taylor was a close friend of Charlotte Brontë, who frequently stayed with the Taylors and described the house and the family in her novel *Shirley*. It is surrounded by nineteenth-century period gardens.

The renovated barn (used by the Taylors in their textile business) has displays illustrating the local textile industry and is the venue for a variety of related activities throughout the year.

Shibden Hall, Godley Lane, Shibden, Halifax HX3 6HG. Telephone: 0422 52246.

The earliest part of this timber-framed

Oakwell Hall, Birstall, built in 1583.

Red House, Gomersal, where Charlotte Brontë frequently stayed.

house dates from about 1420. Shibden Hall has changed over the centuries to accommodate new tastes and different needs and the period room settings here reflect these changes. There is a fine collection of seventeenth- and eighteenth-century furniture and a wealth of period domestic objects.

The hall is set in 90 acres (36 ha) of parkland complete with orienteering course, miniature steam railway, children's playground and tractor train.

Temple Newsam House, Leeds LS15 0AE. Telephone: 0532 647321. 4 miles (6 km) east of Leeds.

'The Hampton Court of the North', Temple Newsam is a magnificent Elizabethan and early Jacobean brick and stone house, set in one of the largest public parks in western Europe. It was the birthplace of Lord Darnley, ill-fated husband of Mary, Queen of Scots, and later the home of the Irwin family.

The house is on a grand scale and surrounds a great courtyard. It contains Leeds City Council's major collections of ceramics, paintings and furniture. The restored long gallery is frequently used for concerts and recitals. There are formal gardens and a home farm (telephone: 0532 645535) stocked with rare breeds of sheep, pigs, cattle, horses and deer.

The grounds, originally landscaped by 'Capability' Brown, are extensive and include a walled rose garden, greenhouses, lakes, terraces, parkland and miles of woodland walks.

7
Museums and galleries

Because of its rich history, West Yorkshire is especially well endowed with museums, which vary in scale from the most impressive civic or national institutions, to specialist and local museums and galleries.

BATLEY

Bagshaw Museum, Wilton Park, Bradford Road, Batley WF17 0AS. Telephone: 0924 472514.

A Gothic mansion built for a local woollen manufacturer in 1875 now houses the Bagshaw Museum. It still retains much of its character, including medieval and pseudo-Egyptian decoration. The displays feature local and natural history, ethnography and fascinating ancient Egyptian and Oriental collections, as well as temporary exhibits.

BRADFORD

Bradford Industrial Museum, Moorside Road, Eccleshill, Bradford BD2 3HP. Telephone: 0274 631756.

Bradford Industrial Museum is situated in a magnificent four-storey woollen mill. Two storeys are so far open to the public and are packed with treasures, most of them relating to the wool industry which made Bradford ('Worstedopolis') world-famous. There are exhibitions concerning Bradford's economic and social history, mill engines, looms and machinery from every period in the history of wool and worsted manufacture, from the earliest days of the industrial revolution to the present time. A transport gallery includes locally made Jowett cars, a steam engine, a tram and the last working trolleybus. (Bradford was the last place in England to have trolleybuses in regular service.) Cross the mill-yard to visit the mill-owner's house furnished in typical high Victorian style, complete with cat asleep on the hearthrug.

Cartwright Hall, Lister Park, Bradford BD9 4NS. Telephone: 0274 493313.

Cartwright Hall is one of the finest art galleries of the region, a magnificent neo-Baroque building opened in 1904 and set in beautiful Lister Park. Its important collection of late Victorian and Edwardian art includes works by Ford Madox Brown, Rossetti, Clausen and Priestman. In its twentieth-century collection are works by Bradford artists William Rothenstein, Edward Wadsworth, Richard Eurich and David Hockney.

The gallery also houses a collection of contemporary prints, many from the Bradford International Print Biennale, and the lower galleries show temporary exhibitions.

Moorside Mill now houses the Bradford Industrial Museum.

Cartwright Hall, Bradford, is a fine art gallery.

Colour Museum, Perkin House, 82 Grattan Road, Bradford BD1 2JB. Telephone: 0274 725138.

This is Britain's only museum devoted to the concept of colour: how we see colour, how it affects our everyday lives, the psychology of colour. Run by the Society of Dyers and Colourists, this fascinating museum has been extended to include many aspects of colour, including the application of dyes and pigments to textiles by dyeing and printing.

National Museum of Photography, Film and Television, Prince's View, Bradford BD5 0TR. Telephone: 0274 727488.

This is one of Britain's most exciting museums. Part of London's Science Museum, it looks at the science, art and history of the visual media: how they work, how they achieve their results and how they affect our lives. Every aspect is covered: from experiments by pioneers like Daguerre and Baird, to the most sophisticated space and microtechnology.

There are changing exhibitions, particularly of photography. The museum helps visitors to examine critically the way newspaper photographs and television influence us.

The museum also contains IMAX, Britain's largest cinema screen, a five-storey high film presentation with six-track stereo that is truly spectacular: an experience not to be missed.

West Yorkshire Transport Museum, Ludlam Street Depot, Mill Lane, off Manchester Road, Bradford BD5 0HG. Telephone: 0274 736006.

The museum houses a collection of mainly, but by no means exclusively, West Yorkshire public service vehicles: double- and single-deck motor buses and coaches, most in original pre-Public Transport Executive liveries, also trams, trolleybuses and railcars.

BRIGHOUSE

Smith Art Gallery, Halifax Road, Brighouse HD6 2AF. Telephone: 0484 719222.

Two small galleries, built about 1900 in a small park, contain the Smith Collection of fine nineteenth-century oil paintings and present a programme of changing exhibitions.

CASTLEFORD

Castleford Museum Room, Castleford Library, Carlton Street, Castleford. Telephone: 0977 559552.

This museum contains a small but important collection of local pottery and glass and Romano-British antiquities from *Lagentium,* the Roman fort which once stood here (see chapter 3).

DEWSBURY

Dewsbury Museum, Crow Nest Park, Heckmondwike Road, Dewsbury. Telephone: 0924 468171.

Dewsbury Museum is housed in the eighteenth-century Crow Nest Mansion and concentrates on the theme of childhood. There are exhibits on children at work (in the fields, textile factories and coal mines), as well as galleries of toys, dolls and other playthings.

FULNECK

Fulneck Moravian Museum, Fulneck, near Pudsey. Telephone: 0532 571440 or 564862.

Fulneck was a small religious settlement established by Moravian settlers in the nineteenth century. The little museum, housed in two eighteenth-century cottages, helps to explain the purpose and work of this immigrant community. There is a Victorian parlour, kitchen, weaving chamber with handloom, and a hand-pumped fire engine.

GOLCAR

Colne Valley Museum, Cliffe Ash, Golcar, Huddersfield. Telephone: 0484 659762.

Near the parish church at Golcar, in the Colne Valley, three converted hillside weavers' cottages provide a fascinating local history display, including the creation of a typical handloom weaver's cottage room of the nineteenth century and a gas-lit clogger's shop of 1910. There are frequent demonstrations of traditional crafts by volunteers: spinning, weaving, clogmaking, lacemaking. The emphasis in the museum is on activity.

HALIFAX

Bankfield Museum, Ackroyd Park, Boothtown Road, Halifax HX3 6HG. Telephone: 0422 54823.

This museum is found in the handsome house of a Halifax mill-owner. Built in the 1860s for Edward Ackroyd in elegant and richly decorated Renaissance style, its very opulence reflects the prosperity of the period. Bankfield has an outstanding collection of costumes, toys, local and natural history as well as the Duke of Wellington's Regimental Museum. It is also the administrative base for the local museums service.

Calderdale Pre-industrial Museum, Piece Hall, Halifax. Telephone: 0422 59031.

Calderdale Industrial Museum, Central Works, Square Road, Halifax. Telephone: 0422 59031.

These two closely related museums can both be reached through Piece Hall, in the centre of Halifax.

The Pre-industrial Museum looks at pre-industrial life and work in Calderdale, covering a period (1450-1830) before the development of the major factories. Halifax was an important centre for handloom weaving and the museum contains examples of spinning wheels, early looms, fulling equipment and exhibits on early worsted cloth manufacturing.

The Industrial Museum takes the story forward and broadens it considerably to include other important Calderdale industries, including engineering. There are working examples of steam and oil-powered engines, carpet looms, toffee-wrapping machines, planing machines and coal and brick-clay mines (complete with gossiping miners and authentic sounds and smells). It was chosen as the Industrial Museum of the Year in 1987.

Horses at Work — National Museum of the Working Horse, Dobbin's Yard, South Parade, Halifax HX1 2LY. Telephone: 0422 46835.

A former Lancashire and Yorkshire Railway goods transhipment yard has been transformed into a remarkable museum devoted to the working horse, once a familiar sight on Britain's streets: from the milkman's pony to the heavy dray horse. Horses and a wide range of carriages and wagons are kept and exhibited on the premises. There are demonstrations of grooming, harnessing and horses working with

Dewsbury Museum is housed in Crow Nest Mansion.

goods drays, passenger vehicles and rare pieces of horse-powered machinery. There is also a gallery of period photographs showing many different aspects of the working horse.

HAWORTH

Brontë Parsonage Museum, Church Street, Haworth, Keighley BD22 8DR. Telephone: 0535 42323.

The parsonage was the home of the three great literary sisters, Charlotte, Emily and Anne Brontë, who lived at Haworth throughout their creative and tragic lives (see chapter 10). The parsonage is kept as close as possible to what it was like when they lived there, with much of their original furniture and many of their personal belongings. The museum, which is run by the Brontë Society, contains manuscripts, letters and portraits, and first editions of the Brontë novels.

Museum of Childhood, West Lane, Haworth, Keighley BD22 8EE. Telephone: 0535 43825.

Childhood memories are evoked by this fascinating museum of toys: dolls, trains, working models, Meccano, games, furniture. It provides pure nostalgia to interest young and old alike.

HEBDEN BRIDGE

Automobilia, Billy Lane, Old Town, Hebden Bridge HX7 8RY. Telephone: 0422 84775.

Automobilia is an impressive collection of vintage cars and motorcycles housed in a former Pennine textile mill. The museum specialises in Morris and Austin cars from the 1920s to 1950s. You will find here the 'James Herriot' car and a 1922 'Bullnose' Morris.

Walkley's Clog Mill, Burnley Road, Hebden Bridge. Telephone: 0422 842061.

Reputed to be the world's only clog factory, this is as much a living workshop as a museum, where you can watch every stage of clogmaking, from raw leather, clog irons and hunks of wood to the finished article. Displays illustrate the history of clogmaking and the various types of clogs, from industrial steel-capped clogs used in many industries to the brightly coloured high-fashion clogs on sale in the showrooms. There is also a refurbished steam engine and an exhibit on the history of steam.

HEPTONSTALL

Heptonstall Museum, Old Grammar School, Churchyard Bottom, Heptonstall. Telephone: 0422 843738.

This is a fine example of a small, traditional seventeenth-century Yorkshire grammar school. Attached to the church, this is where local boys were taught some basic Latin grammar and mathematics, usually by the vicar. Several old desks, benches and school materials survive, plus items of domestic and agricultural interest from the area.

HOLMFIRTH

Holmfirth Postcard Museum, Huddersfield Road, Holmfirth. Telephone: 0484 682231.

The familiar saucy seaside postcard originated at Bamforths of Holmfirth. This museum explores the ideas and creators of the seaside postcards and the background to their popularity at the seaside resorts and northern 'Wakes Weeks', when entire mill-town communities forgot their problems (and their inhibitions). There is a section on the patriotic postcards of the First World War period.

Bamforths also produced magic lantern slides and silent films. The latter are shown regularly in a recreated cinema, while the historical drama of the 1852 Holmfirth flood is depicted on audio-visual display.

HUDDERSFIELD

Huddersfield Art Gallery, Princess Alexandra Walk, Huddersfield. Telephone: 0484 513808.

This gallery houses the Kirklees art collection: a permanent, high-quality collection of paintings, drawings, watercolours and sculptures, mainly British, from the mid nineteenth century to the present. It includes work by L. S. Lowry, Francis Bacon, Henry Moore and Graham Sutherland and a small collection of Japanese prints.

Tolson Memorial Museum, Ravensknowle Park, Wakefield Road, Huddersfield HD5 8DJ. Telephone: 0484 530591 or 541455.

The Tolson Memorial Museum contains Huddersfield's major historic collections and has many items of special interest. There are displays of archaeological finds from nearby Castle Hill (see chapter 3), one of the few surviving examples in Yorkshire of a Pennine packhorse saddle, exhibits on geological and natural history and local transport, industrial material relating to the Huddersfield area, textiles and historic photographs.

ILKLEY

Manor House Museum and Art Gallery, Castle Yard, Ilkley LS29 9DT. Telephone: 09433 600066.

This is a small but interesting museum close to the old Roman fort (see chapter 3), housed in the town's Elizabethan manor house. The museum contains a number of important Roman finds, including altars and pottery, and has displays which interpret the long history of Ilkley, including its emergence in the eighteenth century as a spa for the cure of various ailments.

The Manor House Museum and Art Gallery, Ilkley.

KEIGHLEY

Cliffe Castle, Spring Gardens Lane, Keighley BD20 6LH. Telephone: 0274 758230/1.

Local mill-owners the Butterfields built this grand mansion, which is now a splendid museum of Airedale landscape and life. There are impressive displays of local geology, natural history, minerals and the life of the area, also a suite of restored Victorian reception rooms with magnificent glass chandeliers. In the grounds there are an aviary and attractive gardens.

LEEDS

Abbey House Museum, Abbey Road, Kirkstall, Leeds LS5 3EH. Telephone: 0532 755821.

The twelfth-century gatehouse of Kirkstall Abbey (see chapter 4), which became the home of Leeds ironmasters and their families until the 1920s, has been converted into the city's folk museum. There is an emphasis on Victorian children's toys: card games, mechanical toys, stuffed animals, books. There are also early slot machines (which still work on old pennies) and a street of carefully restored shops, including a pipemaker's, a grocer's, a chemist's, a wheelwright's and the Hark to Rover pub.

Leeds City Art Gallery and Henry Moore Sculpture Study Centre, The Headrow, Leeds LS1 3AA. Telephone: 0532 462495.

This is a major regional art gallery with outstanding collections of nineteenth- and twentieth-century British paintings, French Impressionists and Post-Impressionists and important contemporary work. The new Henry Moore Sculpture Study Centre contains not only major works by the great Castleford-born master but also pieces by many other outstanding British sculptors, including Barbara Hepworth and Jacob Epstein. Also kept here is research and archive material for students of Moore's work. There is a comprehensive art library in the building.

Leeds City Museum, Museum Buildings, The Headrow, Leeds LS1 3AA. Telephone: 0532 462465.

An impressive Italianate building, richly tiled, houses Leeds's main museum, with major collections of Yorkshire geology, natural history and ethnology, and an aquarium. There are rich collections of Mediterranean archaeology, Egyptian mummies, local prehistoric finds, Roman pottery and superb mosaic pavements from the Romano-British settlements at Aldborough, near Boroughbridge.

The Leeds City Museum is linked by the Museum of Leeds Trail with the Leeds Industrial Museum and the Abbey House Museum, Kirkstall. The trail is a 6 mile (10 km) route along the Leeds and Liverpool Canal towpath in the Kirkstall Valley; it passes no less than forty sites of historic interest.

Leeds Industrial Museum, Armley Mills, Canal Road, Leeds LS12 2QF. Telephone: 0532 637861.

When they were built in 1806 between the river Aire and the Leeds and Liverpool Canal, Armley Mills were the biggest in Europe. They now house one of the largest industrial museums in Britain, on several storeys of the building. The exhibits tell the story of Leeds and the wool textile industry, and of the clothing industry of which Leeds is still an important national centre. From the displays of spinning, weaving and carding machinery, the visitor enters a street of Jewish tailors' shops of about 1900, a clothing factory, a buying room. There are a 1930s cinema, one of Europe's few surviving water-powered fulling mills, a waterwheel, presses, steam engines and cranes. During the summer months there are steam engine working days and a boat trip along the canal.

OTLEY

Otley Museum, Civic Centre, Cross Green, Otley. Telephone: 0943 461052.

This is a purely local museum with a wealth of material about the history and archaeology of Otley and Wharfedale, with particular emphasis on the nineteenth century. In the collection are such items as flint tools, local artefacts, old photographs and a Wharfedale printing press. There is also a comprehensive documentary archive.

PONTEFRACT

Pontefract Museum, Salter Row, Pontefract WF8 1BA. Telephone: 0977 797289.

Originally a Carnegie free library, this attractive building in the *art nouveau* style is a popular local museum. It has displays on the history of this medieval town, its royal castle (see chapter 4), featuring a fine early seventeenth-century painting of the castle before the Civil War, and on the local industries, particularly the glassworks and liquorice industry.

RIPPONDEN

Pennine Farm Museum, Ripponden HX4 4DF. Telephone: 0422 54823.

A small farmhouse and adjoining barn near the centre of Ripponden, this museum is set out as a typical Pennine farm of the nineteenth century, with a hill-farmer struggling to make a subsistence income on poor-quality soils and therefore turning to handloom weaving to support the family income. Farm implements, a loom chamber and a small dairy are on display.

SALTAIRE

Victoria Reed Organ Museum, Victoria Hall, Victoria Road, Saltaire, Bradford. Telephone: 0274 585601 (after 5 pm).

This is a unique collection of over 45 instruments, including harmoniums and American organs, as well as the largest English reed organ known and one of the smallest, a little book harmonium. There are also mechanical reed organs; many of the instruments have elaborately carved cases. The organs are demonstrated to visitors and players are allowed to try restored instruments for themselves.

SHIBDEN

West Yorkshire Folk Museum, Shibden Hall, Godley Lane, Shibden, Halifax HX3 6HG. Telephone: 0422 52246. 2 miles (3 km) from Halifax on A58.

The West Yorkshire Folk Museum is adjacent to Shibden Hall (see chapter 6). The seventeenth-century barn houses an important collection of agricultural equipment and implements as well as many different kinds of horse-drawn vehicles, including stage and other coaches, fire engines and a hearse.

The original farm buildings have been transformed into an early nineteenth-century village centre. There is a public house, an estate worker's cottage and workshops for a clogmaker, saddler, blacksmith, wheelwright, potter and basketmaker.

WAKEFIELD

Elizabethan Exhibition Gallery, Brook Street, Wakefield. Telephone: 0924 370211 extension 540 during office hours; 0924 370087 outside office hours.

A fine early grammar school built in the reign of Queen Elizabeth I, this award-winning building has been restored and converted to a gallery for temporary exhibitions. These cover a wide range of topics: art, crafts, photography, history and design.

Wakefield Art Gallery, Wentworth Terrace, Wakefield WF1 3QW. Telephone: 0924 370211 extension 8031 during office hours; 0924 375402 outside office hours.

Wakefield Art Gallery, an attractive Victorian house, once a vicarage, is nationally and internationally known for its important collection of twentieth-century art, including works by Barbara Hepworth and Henry Moore, who were born and brought up in Wakefield and Castleford respectively. There are also fine examples of paintings from both the Camden Town and Bloomsbury groups. There is a small collection of older work, particularly fine paintings of eighteenth- and nineteenth-century Wakefield.

Wakefield Museum, Wood Street, Wakefield WF1 2EV. Telephone: 0924 370211 extension 7190 during office hours; 0924 361767 outside office hours.

Wakefield Museum is housed in a fine early nineteenth-century building originally designed as a music saloon and public rooms and later converted into a mechanics' institute. It is a museum of the local archaeology, history and social history of Wakefield from prehistoric times to the present day. On display are finds from excavations at nearby Sandal Castle (see chapter 4) and Roman Castleford (see chapter 3).

Local prosperity in the eighteenth century is well documented by modern displays on the cloth and corn trade, the mining industry and agriculture. Upstairs can be seen the Waterton Collection of exotic birds and animals collected by the noted nineteenth-century traveller and naturalist Charles Waterton of nearby Walton Hall. There are also seventeenth-century and Victorian period rooms, and a popular collection of dolls and toys.

Yorkshire Mining Museum. See chapter 8.

Yorkshire Sculpture Park, Bretton Hall College of Higher Education, West Bretton, Wakefield WF4 4LG. Telephone: 0924 85302.

The Yorkshire Sculpture Park was founded in 1977 and is now recognised as one of Britain's major art resources. It is set in the beautiful parkland of Bretton Hall. This was originally landscaped in the eighteenth century and provides a varied setting for the exhibitions, permanently sited sculptures and works on loan. The Yorkshire Sculpture Park education and community programmes, sculpture workshops, residencies and exhibitions provide the public with unique opportunities to enjoy and learn about sculpture in the open air.

WEST HARDWICK

Top Farm Agricultural Museum, West Hardwick, near Wakefield WF14 1RG. Telephone: 0977 611165. Signposted off B6428 Featherstone to Fitzwilliam road.

Top Farm is a remarkable collection of farm implements, tractors, tools, threshing machines and ploughs, much of the material collected from local farms and dating back to the closing years of the nineteenth century. There are also vintage cars, wagons, motorcycles, a fairground organ and various animals (including ponies), all in an authentic working farm setting.

'Locking Piece', a fibreglass sculpture by Henry Moore at the Yorkshire Sculpture Park near Wakefield.

8
Industrial history

The industrial revolution was particularly important in West Yorkshire. Many of the high Pennine valleys, with their fast-flowing streams, provided the water power to drive the earliest mills. Later, the development of river navigations and canals (see chapter 9) helped to bring in the vast quantities of raw materials at low prices which fuelled the industrial revolution, particularly in the textile industries of northern England. Much of interest can be seen from this period (1700-1830) and the later Victorian era, which makes West Yorkshire one of the most fascinating areas for anyone interested in Britain's industrial heritage.

Addingham

Though Addingham's early mills have largely vanished or been converted to other uses, the village does contain one fascinating mid eighteenth-century workshop factory (SE 076499). This was where the tradition of cottage handloom weavers working in their own lofts for a yeoman clothier began to yield to workers weaving alongside each other in a common floor or loft: the world's first 'manufactories'.

The Piece Hall, Halifax.

Heptonstall. Reached by a minor road from Hebden Bridge.

This is a perfect example of a hilltop weavers' settlement, pre-dating the industrial revolution, with seventeenth- and eighteenth-century weavers' cottages. There is a cloth hall, where fabric was bought and sold; this was built in 1545 and was the only one in the region for more than a century. A medieval cobbled track, 'The Buttress', still runs steeply down the hillside to Hebden Bridge.

The nearby valleys (for example, Colden Water, Grimsworth Dean, Hardcastle Crags, Jumble Clough) are filled with the remains of early mills and watercourses, many of them having their origins in monastic times and contributing to the birth of the industrial revolution.

Jack Metcalfe's Turnpike Road (SE 023102). Reached by footpath behind the Great Western Hotel on A62.

One of the earliest engineered highways across the Pennines was built in 1759 by Blind Jack Metcalfe, the great Knaresborough road engineer, across Standedge. Metcalfe first developed the technique of 'floating' the metalled road over bog land on a raft of brushwood and heather bundles: a technique used later by George Stephenson on the Liverpool-Manchester railway.

Kirkstall Valley, Leeds.

The area from the canal basin in the centre of Leeds to Kirkstall Abbey is one which is particularly rich in early industrial remains, now interpreted as part of the Museum of Leeds Trail (see chapter 7). At Kirkstall Forge, not far from the abbey (see chapter 4) steelmaking and engineering continue on a site founded by the Cistercian brothers in late monastic times. This perhaps makes this the site with the longest continuous tradition of industrial use in western Europe.

Luddites

Any study of the industrial history of the region must include reference to the Luddites of West Yorkshire: the weavers who, in the 1830s, smashed the new power looms to

The statue of Sir Titus Salt at Saltaire.

The Unitarian church at Saltaire.

protect their own jobs, with consequent riots, military action and loss of life. Mills and mill communities in and around the Colne and Spen valleys were severely affected. Many places with Luddite associations still survive, including the pubs where the plotters met. See Phyllis Bentley's powerful novel *Inheritance* and the 'Luddite Trail' (on sale in most tourist information centres).

Lumbutts and Mankinholes. Reached by following the A6033 south from Todmorden towards Littleborough, before turning sharp right beyond Walsden, signposted to Lumbutts.

At Lumbutts is a curious water-powered textile mill, which once consisted of three waterwheels, one on top of the other, fed by a series of dams operating in siphon. The water tower remains (SD 957235). Mankinholes is a fascinating hillside weavers' settlement.

Marsden Moor

Much of this National Trust owned moorland area is riddled with shafts and workings linked to the construction of the great canal tunnel under the moorland. It represents, in its own right, an important area of industrial archaeology. This interesting area can be explored following the Standedge Trail available from Tunnel End Centre, Marsden (see chapter 2).

Micklethwaite. Reached by taking Micklethwaite Lane off the A650 Bingley to Keighley road, turning left into Beck Road to Holroyd Mill.

Holroyd Mill, a typical early nineteenth-century woollen mill on the banks of Morton Beck, on the Airedale side of Rombalds Moor, forms part of a conservation area of a typical mill village community. The mill has been developed as a craft centre, Micklethwaite Studio Workshops, with jewellers, potters, designers and furniture makers re-using the old mill premises.

Nutclough Mill, Hebden Bridge.

The world's first producer co-operative was founded in 1870 and run on profit-sharing lines as the Hebden Bridge Fustian Manufacturing Co-operative Society until 1918 when it was sold to the Co-operative Wholesale Society (which still has a mill in Hebden Bridge). One of the founders of the Nutclough society was Robert Halstead, who later helped to found the Workers' Educational Association in 1903.

Piece Hall, Halifax.

Halifax's magnificent Piece Hall, where clothiers and merchants brought their 'pieces' of cloth for sale, was built in 1775 to the design of Thomas Bradley. Its magnificent two-storeyed colonnades around a huge rectangular piazza create a splendid sense of space and elegance. It is now the home of Calderdale's Pre-industrial Museum (see chapter 7).

Saltaire

Developed in the 1850s, Sir Titus Salt's astonishing 'model' mill village on the river Aire was built to enable the factory and workforce to move away from the slums and pollution of inner Bradford. At its peak the great canalside mill held 1200 looms capable of weaving 30,000 yards (9100 metres) of cloth every day and employed over three thousand people. Around the mill with its Venetian campanile-style chimney, Salt developed a village which catered as much for spiritual as physical needs. There was the elegantly beautiful Congregational church, a town hall, a school, a mechanics' institute, almshouses for retired workers, a riverside park (in which swearing and gambling were not permitted) and, significantly, no public house.

The rows of well proportioned workers' houses, in streets named after members of the Salt family, are now sought-after dwellings and a tribute to the vision of their creator. His statue stands in the park above those of a llama and an alpaca, the importation and the spinning of whose fleeces made his fortune.

The little boathouse by the river is now a Victorian restaurant: visitors can take a boat on the river or enjoy the atmosphere of a typical Victorian parlour. There is also the Victoria Reed Organ Museum (see chapter 7) and the Shipley Glen Tramway (see chapter 9). Saltaire station in the centre of the village has been restored in period style and reopened, with frequent trains on the Airedale Line from Leeds and Bradford to Keighley (see chapter 9).

Sowerby Bridge

A complex of early industrial revolution factories are now being restored around the Calder and Hebble/Rochdale Canal Basin as part of the Sowerby Bridge Riverside Scheme. They will be developed into a major industrial heritage area.

Thwaites Mill (SE 328313). Between Leeds and Rothwell off the A61 near Stourton.

This remarkable mid nineteenth-century water-powered putty mill on the river Aire south of Leeds is in the process of restoration as a visitor centre.

Tong-Cockersdale

This is an area of old iron-mine, coal-pit and fireclay workings between Leeds and Bradford. It includes the lines of many narrow-gauge and industrial railways, now abandoned and grassed over, which form part of a country park (see chapter 2). It is an area rich in the industrial archaeology of the early nineteenth century.

Yorkshire Mining Museum, Caphouse Colliery, New Road, Overton, Wakefield WF4 4RH. Telephone: 0924 848806.

Opened in June 1988, the Yorkshire Mining Museum is located on the site of Caphouse Colliery. The shaft dates back to 1791, and a history of methods and conditions of mining from the early 1800s to the present day is illustrated by an extensive underground tour, innovative indoor display area and comprehensive outdoor exhibits. Picnic area, nature trail, rope-haul railway and education facilities are also available.

The Huddersfield Narrow Canal enters Standedge Tunnel at the Tunnel End Canal and Countryside Centre, Marsden.

9
Canals and railways

The canals and railways of West Yorkshire are integral parts of the industrial heritage of the region. Precisely because the car and the lorry have taken so much traffic away from the waterway and rail systems in post-war years, the neglect of their immediate environs has often allowed them to become areas of historic interest, with many buildings, bridges and artefacts of great value surviving destruction.

Areas that were once industrial wastelands have, after half a century, been reclaimed by nature. Birch trees, in particular, have recolonised old sidings and wharfs, giving them a new green covering. In many cases, this has been assisted by tidying and replanting schemes. This is particularly true of the trans-Pennine canals, which in West Yorkshire are going through a remarkable period of rebirth and discovery.

CANALS

Aire and Calder Navigation

The difference between a navigation and a canal is that a navigation is primarily an improved river, deepened and straightened to make it easier for the passage of boats, but with frequent stretches of locks and canal to bypass natural or man-made obstructions such as weirs. Because they have been subject to improvement over a long period, particularly since the eighteenth century, a navigation may be mostly canal and have little natural river component left. However, it can be subject to forceful currents on its river sections, compared with the still waters of a canal, making larger and more powerful boats essential.

The Aire and Calder Navigation, which leads up from the main Humber estuary at Goole, is an extremely old waterway but is still a busy commercial route with bulk cargoes of coal, oil and grain carried in powerful barges and the traditional tug-hauled 'Tom Pudding' containers. It is not generally realised that Leeds is an inland port: the canal basin (behind the station) and the old wharves are now being revitalised as part of a new Leeds Waterfront. It is possible to walk along the towpath, through a heavily industrialised landscape in the lower Aire Valley, which nevertheless has much of interest. There is also a branch of the canal to Wakefield which, in the Wakefield Canal Basin (just off the Barnsley road), links with the Calder and Hebble Navigation.

Calder and Hebble Navigation

This waterway was opened in 1779, linking Wakefield and the Aire and Calder with the upper Calder valley as far as Halifax and Sowerby Bridge. Though traversing a predominantly industrial landscape, there are some delightful rural stretches, particularly around Durkar, Elland and Horbury, whilst Mirfield with its boatyards and Brighouse with its canal basin are rich in canal history.

There is a pleasant stretch around Salterhebble locks, below Halifax, where a long-vanished branch served Halifax, and Sowerby Bridge Basin itself has attractive canal warehouses and pubs.

There is a waterbus and floating restaurant boat service between Mirfield and Brighouse during the summer. Boats can be hired for cruising holidays on the Calder and Hebble.

Huddersfield Broad Canal

This is a 3½ mile (6 km) section of canal which links the centre of Huddersfield with the Calder and Hebble Navigation along the Colne Valley.

Huddersfield Narrow Canal

The Huddersfield Narrow Canal runs from the Tame Valley, in Greater Manchester, through the great Standedge Tunnel (the highest and longest canal tunnel in the British Isles) to Marsden and the Colne Valley, where it is linked with the Huddersfield Broad Canal and subsequently the Calder and Hebble, in Huddersfield.

Opened in 1811, it took seventeen years to build and was an epic engineering achievement, requiring technological innovation in the creation of the 3 mile (5 km) tunnel under Standedge. Like the Rochdale Canal, this canal was abandoned: in 1944 the tunnel was closed, locks were 'cascaded' and many sections filled in. With the help of a voluntary body, the Huddersfield Narrow Canal Society, and after much hard work, including physical labour digging and restoring locks, and with the financial support of local councils and the Manpower Services Commission, extensive lengths of the canal have been reopened, with a regular trip-boat service operating from Uppermill on the Greater Manchester side.

The key question, however, concerns the canal tunnel, a nationally important monument to the canal age in its own right. If it can be made safe for navigation, it can perhaps be developed into a major tourist attraction.

At Tunnel End Canal and Countryside Centre (Reddisher Road, Marsden; telephone 0484 846062) there is a fascinating exhibition telling the story of the canal and the intriguing developments around it. The Standedge Trail is a series of walking routes over the pass, including the 'Boat Lane' used by boat horses when men were legging their boats through the tunnel itself.

Leeds and Liverpool Canal

This is West Yorkshire's oldest canal and the only trans-Pennine canal still open for through navigation (though the Rochdale and Huddersfield Narrow canals may eventually be reopened).

The section of this canal within West Yorkshire, linking the Aire and Calder Basin in Leeds with Shipley, Bingley and Skipton, was opened, in stages, during the 1770s, though the full canal route across the Pennines to Liverpool was not opened until 1816 owing to financial crises caused by the Napoleonic Wars. The Bradford branch, which played an important part in the development of the city and which ran directly into the city centre, was closed before the Second World War and has almost completely vanished except for the name of 'Canal Road' leading out of the city.

The Leeds to Liverpool canal is a magnificent waterway, following the older 'contour' canal principle of taking a longer route following the natural contours of the land (in this case the Aire Gap through the Pennines) to avoid heavy engineering and locking.

Though commercial traffic disappeared many years ago, this remains a popular cruise waterway, whilst the towpath offers a delightful walking route through Airedale. Because the canal parallels the former turnpike road and railway line, you are never far away from a bus route or railway station, making it an ideal way of taking an easy, fairly level stroll.

The route between Leeds and Rodley is part of the Museum of Leeds Trail (see chapter 7), but beyond here unfolds a superb area of almost hidden green and wooded countryside: through Rodley, Newlay, Calverley, Esholt and Shipley, the finest unspoiled part of Airedale. Though Shipley is built up, you are soon in the great canyon between Salt's Mill at Saltaire and another delightful semi-rural stretch past Hurst Wood to Bingley, crossing a fine aqueduct over the river Aire.

Bingley, with its many canalside wharves and warehouses, is rich in history, and the two famous staircase locks, Three Rise and the spectacular Five Rise Locks, a wonder of canal engineering, provide a place to linger. Much of the original lock machinery is still *in situ,* a working museum of eighteenth-century canal technology. Between Bingley and Kildwick, the canal follows an elevated section with fine views across the Aire Valley, going through Silsden, another typical Pennine canal and mill town.

A waterbus service is operated in the summer months between Shipley and Bingley, via Saltaire. Narrowboats can be hired for cruising holidays.

Rochdale Canal

Originally surveyed by James Brindley and engineered by William Jessup, the Rochdale Canal, opened in 1804, runs from the centre of Manchester to Rochdale, before cutting across the Calder gap from Littleborough and Todmorden. It then follows the little river Calder to its junction with the Calder and Hebble at Sowerby Bridge, where it has been closed and filled in. Though this was the shortest route between the mills of Calderdale, heavy locking required time and water and the canal finally succumbed to road competition by 1939, though some stretches remained in use after the Second World War. It was finally abandoned in 1952.

Owing to the efforts of the Rochdale Canal Society, West Yorkshire County Council and Calderdale Council, much of the canal has now been reopened in stages, with new lock gates and bridges to remove blockages. The canal is open from beyond Todmorden to Mytholmroyd, and nowhere has felt the benefit more than Hebden Bridge, where a jumble of derelict sheds has been cleared to create a magnificent new marina. Formidable obstacles remain but, given the energy and determination of the canal enthusiasts, there seems little doubt that this beautiful and dramatic waterway, the most direct route by boat across the Pennines, will be restored throughout its length, with important tourism and economic benefits to the Calder Valley. In the meantime, the towpath remains a delightful walkway.

A waterbus has returned on one of the loveliest sections of the canal, between Hebden Bridge and Callis Wood, and sometimes right through to Todmorden. Horse-drawn boats are used on certain occasions.

RAILWAYS

The railways of West Yorkshire are as much part of the region's heritage as the canals, with the advantage that most of them are still in use. Whilst West Yorkshire's railways have a major and growing importance as a means of getting people to and around the region (new high-speed electric trains operate to Wakefield and Leeds), several of the local lines offer a wonderful way of seeing the county. Here are a selection of rail routes in West Yorkshire which are of particular historic or scenic interest.

Airedale Line

The line through the Aire Valley, branching at Shipley into Bradford Forster Square, was originally the Leeds and Bradford Railway before being taken over by the mighty Midland Railway on its route to Scotland. It is in a real sense the true Brontë line, having been used by Charlotte and Anne on their last sad journey from Keighley to Scarborough in 1849. It is scenically very fine, like the canal avoiding the ribbon development that defaces much of the valley.

Caldervale Line

George Stephenson himself was responsible for building the impressive railway through the Calder Valley in the 1840s. Originally known as the Manchester and Leeds Railway, it included the 1 mile (1.5 km) long Summit Tunnel between Todmorden and Littleborough. When, in December 1984, an oil train exploded, sending huge flames hundreds of feet high through the brick ventilators, the excellence of the railway builders was proved, because, although major repairs were needed, the tunnel survived.

It remains a scenically impressive route, particularly between Halifax and Todmorden, where it winds its way through the high crags

A steam train at Haworth station on the Keighley and Worth Valley Railway.

of the Calder Valley. The line between Hebden Bridge and Burnley (the Roses Link), which climbs through Cliviger Gorge, also offers a fine journey.

Harrogate Line

Though only a short length of this line is within West Yorkshire, the steep climb through Headingley and Horsforth to Bramhope Tunnel offers a startling contrast between predominantly suburban landscapes and the magnificent open countryside of Wharfedale, as the train emerges from the tunnel portals to cross Arthington Viaduct over the Wharfe *en route* to Harrogate.

Keighley and Worth Valley Railway, Haworth Station, Keighley BD22 8NJ. Telephone: 0535 45214; talking timetable 0535 43629.

The Keighley and Worth Valley Railway, a 4½ mile (7 km) branch line between Keighley, Haworth and Oxenhope, is one of the region's top tourist attractions. Every weekend, and daily during July and August and at other peak holiday times, steam trains, lovingly restored, chug up the valley, calling at stations whose restoration has an attention to detail which borders on the fanatical: from the milk churns and luggage on the platform to the porter's collar studs.

Because this railway has been used for so many film and television settings, most notably *The Railway Children* and *Yanks,* it may have an unconscious familiarity to the visitor, but it is a proper public transport service providing trains for local communities and bringing many thousands of visitors to Haworth. Keighley and Worth Valley trains interlink with British Rail Airedale Line services and through booking facilities are available.

In the museum at Oxenhope there is a major collection of steam locomotives, a wide range of main-line freight and passenger trains, as well as some industrial locomotives.

Leeds to Selby railway

This is Yorkshire's oldest railway still in continuous passenger use, being part of the Leeds to Hull line. Opened in 1834, it was, in many ways, just as important as its more famous predecessors, the Stockton and Darlington (1825) and the Liverpool and Manchester (1830), because of its remarkable innovative civil engineering techniques, including the development of cost-saving skew bridges that were to be a pattern for civil engineering to come.

Many original features of the 1834 line have survived, including the great brick cuttings at Marsh Lane (near the site of the original station) east of Leeds, Micklefield, with its original 1830s stationmaster's house and porter's room, and South Milford, with its rare, low-level 1834 station, which is still in use: possibly the oldest working station in the world.

Middleton Railway, Moor Road, Hunslet, Leeds.

The Middleton Railway claims to be the world's oldest railway. It was the first to be authorised by Act of Parliament to transport coal from mines in Middleton (south Leeds) to wharves on the Aire and Calder Navigation, and the first, in 1812, to use steam traction on a regular commercial basis, the locomotives devised by the great Leeds engineers Matthew Murray and John Blenkinsop. Each Murray-Blenkinsop engine was claimed to do the work of sixteen horses and eight men. Little wonder that their ideas were copied and developed so brilliantly by George Stephenson when designing many of his own locomotives, including the famed *Rocket.*

The Middleton Railway Trust now operates steam trains over much of the original line at weekends and holiday times.

Penistone Line

The direct railway route between Huddersfield and Sheffield through the South Pennines and the edge of the Peak District has narrowly escaped closure in recent years. It deserves to be far better known as a highly scenic route through the Holme Valley into a richly wooded part of South Yorkshire. The many stations offer excellent opportunities for the rambler.

Shipley Glen Tramway, Saltaire. Telephone: 0274 589010.

Shipley Glen Tramway is a rope-hauled funicular railway. This unique Victorian inclined railway was built to link the village of Saltaire (across Roberts Park) with the pleasure gardens at the top of Shipley Glen.

Restored to modern standards of safety, the railway's brightly coloured open-air cars ascend and descend the little wooded valley to provide an unusual and nostalgic ride. It operates at weekends and holiday times from spring to autumn.

Wharfedale Line

The twin routes, from Leeds and Bradford Forster Square, which leave the Airedale Line to cross the watershed into Wharfedale did much to establish Ilkley as an inland spa and popular commuter town. Both routes (the lines join at Guiseley) provide the most scenic rail journeys purely within West Yorkshire, crossing into the rich, rolling landscape of the Yorkshire Dales, with open views of moorland and valley landscape. The local stations offer delightful walking routes from one to the next.

10 Famous people

West Yorkshire has, over the centuries, produced many remarkable personalities who have achieved national, and in some cases international, fame in their chosen fields.

William Congreve (1670-1729) was born in Bardsey, near Wetherby, and became a celebrated playwright. His *Way of the World* is still enjoyed for its cynical view of life at the time of William and Mary.

The Brontë sisters are perhaps the most famous people to have been born in West Yorkshire, though they were of Irish/Cornish parentage. Perhaps the blend of Celtic imagination and Yorkshire realism produced that explosion of extraordinary talent in the parsonage of what was, in the 1830s and 1840s, a raw, expanding industrial town, Haworth. *Wuthering Heights* by **Emily Brontë** (1818-48) is one of the masterpieces of English literature. **Charlotte Brontë** (1816-55), whose *Jane Eyre* remains one of the most popular novels in the language, whilst not possessing the genius of Emily, was nevertheless a writer of the highest calibre. Her novels remain important social documents of Victorian life. **Anne Brontë** (1820-49) is undeservedly neglected, though her *Tenant of Wildfell Hall* is a fine and moving book.

Contrary to popular misconception, the girls and their ill-fated brother Branwell were not born in Haworth, but in Thornton, near Bradford. There is a display, including facsimiles of their birth registers, in Thornton church. Although this church is not the original building, the ruins of the medieval church in which they were christened can be seen nearby.

The family moved to Haworth in 1820 and the Parsonage Museum (see chapter 7) has restored the rooms and conserved relics much as they would have known them. Though Haworth church has been transformed since their time, the graves of Branwell, Emily and Charlotte are there. Anne is buried in Scarborough.

However, the real memorial to the Brontës' genius is the landscape, so perfectly captured in Emily's work. The favourite moorland walk is to the waterfall now known as Brontë Falls or higher to Top Withins Farm, the place which undoubtedly inspired *Wuthering Heights*.

Other writers have drawn deep inspiration from the Yorkshire landscape. **Dr Phyllis Bentley** (1894-1977), who grew up in the Spen Valley, transmitted in her novel *Inheritance* the feeling and flavour of life in a textile community from the early years of the industrial revolution, when the Luddites smashed the weaving frames with hammers, to the 1950s.

The most popular and most widely recognised Yorkshire novelist, playwright and personality of the twentieth century was **J. B. Priestley** (1894-1984), born in Bradford, whose fictional 'Bruddersford' in *The Good Companions,* with its hero Jess Oakroyd, has immortalised the region of his birth and the character of its people. Although his was a love-hate relationship with Bradford, no one has described the city more perceptively and sympathetically than he did in his *English Journey* of 1934. His plays, too, introduce the character of the blunt Yorkshireman, or, as in *Eden's End,* vividly capture the suburban comforts of Edwardian Ilkley. A massive bronze statue of Priestley now stands outside the National Museum of Photography, Film and Television in Bradford.

West Yorkshire continues to breed writers of talent. The Poet Laureate, **Ted Hughes,** was born in Mytholmroyd; in much of his early verse he powerfully captures the bleak Calderdale landscape. His former wife, the American poetess and novelist **Sylvia Plath** (1932-63),

The birthplace of the Brontë sisters at Thornton.

also described the Pennine landscape in verse of force and beauty before she died, tragically young. She is buried in Heptonstall churchyard.

A young Bingley librarian, **John Braine,** shot to national fame with a powerful novel, *Room at the Top,* which categorised him as one of the 'angry young men' of his generation. This was a moving and unsentimental story of a working-class lad's ruthless rise in a typical small Yorkshire town. At the other side of the county the Ossett writer **Stan Barstow** enjoyed equal success in the early 1960s with *A Kind of Loving,* a haunting story of the realities of teenage love. Unlike John Braine, Barstow has never left his roots and has continued to chronicle the life of the people of the region in novels of great integrity, including *Joby,* a sharply observed study of adolescence.

West Yorkshire has a remarkable music-making tradition which embraces such nationally known ensembles as the Huddersfield Choral Society and the Leeds Philharmonic, and such famous brass bands as the Black Dyke and the Brighouse and Rastrick, but only one international composer, **Frederick Delius** (1862-1934), born in Bradford of German parents. Although he left for such exotic climes as the West Indies and France as soon as he was able, Delius had a deep fondness for the Yorkshire countryside and his *Northern Sketches,* composed in his youth, were reputedly inspired by walks on Ilkley Moor.

The statue of Thomas Chippendale at Otley.

The visual arts, however, have fared better. **Thomas Chippendale** (1719-79), one of the world's greatest cabinet-makers, was born in Otley and much of his work can be seen in the county at Harewood House and Nostell Priory (see chapter 6).

The twentieth century has produced two world-famous sculptors: **Henry Moore,** born in Castleford the son of a coal-miner, and **Barbara Hepworth,** from Wakefield. Both have left important legacies to their native region: in the Henry Moore Sculpture Gallery which the great man helped to establish and endow before his death (he was particularly concerned to offer young sculptors study facilities) and Barbara Hepworth with her *Family of Man* in the Yorkshire Sculpture Park at Bretton and elsewhere in Wakefield (see chapter 7).

Another artist from the region to achieve international recognition is Bradford-born painter and designer **David Hockney,** whose shimmering canvases are sought after throughout the world.

West Yorkshire has also had its share of political figures: **Herbert Asquith** (Prime Minister 1908-16) was born in Morley, whilst **Harold Wilson** (Prime Minister 1964-70, 1974-6) came from Huddersfield.

In terms of science, West Yorkshire's greatest figure was undoubtedly **Joseph Priestley** (1733-1804), discoverer of oxygen, who was born in Birstall, near Leeds, educated at Batley Grammar School and was minister at the little Unitarian chapel in City Square, Leeds, between 1767 and 1773.

However, it was engineers who were to make their mark on the city's growing industry, men like **John Smeaton** (1724-94), creator of the Eddystone Lighthouse and much more besides, born (and buried) in Whitkirk, Leeds, and **John Blenkinsop** and **Matthew Murray,** whose cast-iron memorial, made by a grateful workforce, stands in a former churchyard, in Holbeck, a Leeds inner suburb.

Two great names of modern science are from West Yorkshire. **Sir John Cockroft,** who received the Nobel Prize in 1912 for splitting the atom, was born in Todmorden, whilst the physicist and astronomer **Sir Fred Hoyle** was born in Baildon, near Bradford, and educated at Bingley Grammar School.

11
Towns and villages

Because West Yorkshire is such a heavily and densely populated region, it is possible only to give a selection of the many towns and villages worth visiting and the variety of things to do and see there.

ABERFORD

This is a virtually unspoiled eighteenth-century coaching town, formerly on the Great North Road (A1), now mercifully bypassed. It has a couple of fine old coaching inns, an attractive main street, a ruined windmill and superb Gothic almshouses, built by the Gascoigne family and now a crafts centre open to the public. A short walk from Aberford, through Parlington Park, is a great triumphal arch erected in 1783 to celebrate the American War of Independence, inscribed 'Liberty in North America triumphant'.

ACKWORTH

This village is famous for its Quaker school, with some delightful eighteenth- and nineteenth-century houses and cottages. The church is Victorian and there are some fine eighteenth-century almshouses. A plague stone stands at the road junction just beyond the village: this was where villagers left money in exchange for food.

BADSWORTH

Badsworth is a village of character, with a fine medieval church, attractive old houses and a good planting of trees. From Upton Beacon, to the south of the village, the Lincolnshire Wolds and the Derbyshire Peak District can be seen.

BARDSEY

This lower Wharfedale village has three claims to fame: an Anglo-Saxon church (see chapter 5), the birthplace of Congreve (see chapter 10) and the Bingley Arms (on the Leeds to Wetherby road), reputed to be England's oldest pub, with documented records of brewers and innkeepers going back to AD 1000. The inn has two priests' holes and a Dutch oven.

BATLEY

Hardly a tourist town in the conventional sense, Batley is not without interest. There is a cobbled market place, a handsome town hall and a library with a celebrated clock which once belonged to the market hall. The Central Chapel in the Square, built in 1869, was known as the 'Shoddy Temple' because of the amount of business done by local textile merchants on the chapel steps after Sunday morning service. 'Shoddy' is a cloth made from old rags reworked with new wool, a technique of recycling material to make a cheaper cloth which became a major industry in the Batley and Dewsbury areas (though the word now has undeserved connotations of inferior quality). The technique was developed by Benjamin Law of nearby Gomersal, the 'Shoddy King', who lies buried in Batley churchyard.

Wilton Park, a pleasant 41 acre (17 ha) park in Batley, with a lake and gardens, houses the fine Bagshaw Museum (see chapter 7).

BINGLEY

Bingley is an ancient Airedale town, which still retains much of its character, particularly around its early Tudor church (with a fine Burne-Jones window) and seventeenth-century Old White Horse Inn. Buried in the churchyard is John Nicholson (1790-1843), the Airedale poet, who died when he fell off stepping stones into the river Aire after returning home from a drinking spree. The fine Victorian Myrtle Park comes almost into the town centre and extends down to a footbridge over the river Aire. Here riverside

The Bagshaw Museum, Batley.

The Old White Horse Inn at Bingley.

paths lead to the historic Beckfoot packhorse bridge which crosses Harden Beck, whilst other routes climb to St Ives and through the wooded Aire gorge (see chapter 2). Bingley has perhaps the most spectacular section of the Leeds and Liverpool Canal: around Three Rise and Five Rise locks (see chapter 9).

BOSTON SPA

Boston Spa, the 'Little Cheltenham of Yorkshire', is a small but gracious town on the banks of the river Wharfe. It was established in Georgian times when Magnesian limestone and sulphur springs were discovered close to the new turnpike road between Otley and Tadcaster. Gentlemen and ladies came in their carriages to drink and bathe in the medicinal waters, said to be excellent for gout and rheumatism. By the nineteenth century, the growth of Harrogate with its huge variety of mineral waters and facilities eclipsed Boston Spa, but its beautiful creamy-coloured stone houses and inns remain. There is a fine bridge over the river and pleasant riverside walks past the Old Baths, now a fishing centre. **Thorpe Arch**, a separate village on the other side of the bridge, has attractive houses, cottages and village greens.

BRADFORD

In the middle ages Bradford was a small town around Bradford Beck with a corn and fulling mill, tanners, stonemasons, iron-workers, innkeepers and its own supply of coal. Such streets as Kirkgate, Ivegate and Westgate ('gate' being northern dialect for street) date from this period. By the time of Henry VIII the town was already well known for its clothing industry. In the Civil War Bradford was strongly Parliamentarian and it was twice held by Royalists under siege. During the second siege the Parliamentary General Fairfax's wife was held hostage near the present Cock and Bottle Inn.

In the eighteenth century the woollen trade prospered and the city began to specialise in the production of high-quality woollen yarns. This trade was given impetus with the arrival of better roads in the form of turnpikes, the opening of the Bradford branch of the Leeds and Liverpool Canal in 1774 and the establishment of a bank to provide funds for new enterprises.

In 1798 Messrs Ramsbottom, Swaine and Murgatroyd built the first steam-powered mill on the corner of Westholme Street and Thornton Road. Though this mill no longer stands, its building was a major turning point in Bradford's history. Wool and steam power created the 'Bradford miracle', the dawning of a new era of wealth and prosperity, but the end of the small town lying in the hollow. The population of a mere 1600 in 1810 exploded to 103,768 in 1851, with a huge influx of workers, many of them Irish, to man the new mills. Such dramatic expansion brought equally dramatic problems, with the growth of overcrowded slums to house the new workforce. A Sanitary Report of 1844 highlighted Bradford as one of the most squalid towns in Britain, with no proper sewage system or water supply, and appalling diseases and social difficulties.

Improvement soon came, with Bradford emerging as a leader in terms of reforming zeal and radicalism. Not only were the slums cleared and such model villages as Saltaire (see chapter 8) established, but Bradford entered a period of civic expansion and pride, much of which still leaves its mark on the city. The new princes of industry built magnificent, Renaissance-style mills, such as Lister's Mill at Manningham (which still produces world-famous velvets), Milligan and Forbes's warehouse in Hall Ings (now the *Telegraph and Argus* building) and the remarkable area of warehouses behind the cathedral known as 'Little Germany'. It was so named because of close trade links with Germany and the number of German merchants (such as Frederick Delius's father, whose warehouse still stands) who lived in the city. This area of Bradford exists to this day: a 'Little Germany Trail' guide can be purchased at the tourist information centre.

No buildings better symbolise Bradford at the height of its economic power and fortune than the great City Hall, erected in 1873 in elaborate, richly decorated thirteenth-century

Left: *Lister's Mill at Manningham, Bradford.*
Below: *The Alhambra Theatre, Bradford.*

Gothic style by the architects Lockwood and Mawson, or the neo-classical St George's Hall, built to the design of the same architects twenty years earlier, and now one of the finest concert halls in the region. Another splendid building is the Wool Exchange, built in 1867 at a time when Bradford ('Worstedopolis') dominated the world's wool trade and prices determined there were followed everywhere.

Though Bradford has suffered catastrophic economic decline there is clear evidence of the city determinedly 'bouncing back' with a revival of the wool industry, particularly in export markets, and a growth of tourism. Though a great disservice was done to the city by poor-quality development, including city centre 'ring' roads and the destruction of much of the Victorian heritage, a great amount remains. The city is now pursuing a policy of pedestrianising the centre and restoring many buildings: for example, the Alhambra Theatre, a superb Edwardian building now magnificently returned to former glories. The University of Bradford, a relative newcomer to the academic scene, already has an international reputation in the applied sciences. Bradford is also becoming an important centre for the arts. Town trails, available from the tourist information centre, now help the visitor to discover what is still, in many respects, West Yorkshire's grandest Victorian city.

BRAMHAM

A delightful stone village consisting of eighteenth- and early nineteenth-century houses, an inn and a medieval church with a Norman tower, Bramham is set in beautiful, rolling countryside, close to but bypassed by the Great North Road. Bramham Park, one of the finest eighteenth-century houses in the region (see chapter 6) is nearby.

BRIGHOUSE

Brighouse has always been an important crossroads of the Pennines, lying as it does between the larger towns of Bradford, Halifax, Huddersfield and Leeds. Improvements to the Calder and Hebble Canal by the Leeds engineer John Smeaton in 1779 and the later arm of 1834, which created the canal basin in the town centre, gave great stimulus to trade, particularly to textiles and textile engineering. Now bypassed by through traffic, Brighouse's town centre is largely pedestrianised, allowing the visitor to explore its interesting, mainly Victorian, buildings. The Smith Art Gallery (see chapter 7), close to the town centre, has an interesting collection of nineteenth-century, mainly landscape, paintings.

DENBY DALE

A pleasant village at the top end of the Holme Valley, in attractive countryside, and dominated by the long railway viaduct on the Penistone Line (see chapter 9), Denby Dale's claim to fame is for the production of giant meat pies, a tradition which began in 1788 and which is revived every few years. The last one, baked in 1964, was 18 feet (5½ metres) long and weighed 6½ tons (6600 kg). The dish now stands outside the village hall.

DEWSBURY

Market days Wednesday and Saturday.

The capital of Yorkshire's famed 'heavy woollen' district, Dewsbury is still full of mills and warehouses, though many have closed and been put to other uses, and those that remain are highly mechanised, employing far fewer people than in the past.

Dewsbury is one of the region's oldest towns, centre of a large and ancient parish (see chapter 5). According to legend, St Paulinus preached here in AD 627 on the site of the present parish church and baptised converts in the river Calder. Patrick Brontë, father of the famous sisters, was curate here in 1809-11 and Charlotte taught at Healds House School on Dewsbury Moor, run by Miss Wooler. In the nineteenth century Dewsbury, like Batley, became closely associated with the 'shoddy' industry and also with coal mining.

ELLAND

The name of this old town comes from 'ea-land', meaning 'land by water': the river Calder. It also gave its name to the Ealands, a powerful local family murdered in a bitter feud, though their descendants on the female side, the Savilles, have played a prominent part in West Yorkshire life ever since.

A jumble of streets round the town centre marks the medieval town, which grew rapidly in the eighteenth and nineteenth centuries around the Calder and Hebble Canal. Though it is predominantly a textile town (Gannex raincoats are made here), sweets became an important sideline with the establishment of several firms, including Joseph Dobson's factory in Northgate in 1850. Dobson's still make such traditional boiled sweets as 'Yorkshire Mixture' and the familiar humbugs. The company opens its doors to pre-booked parties to see traditional sweetmaking (telephone: 0422 72165).

There are in Elland pleasant parks, riverside and canalside areas, interesting buildings and a choice of walks from the town.

GOOSE EYE

This is a compact mill hamlet tucked into a deep-sided valley on the outskirts of Keighley, celebrated for its Turkey Inn which brews its own 'Goose Eye' beer.

HALIFAX

One of the oldest of West Yorkshire towns, Halifax has a history going back well into medieval times. In the thirteenth century Halifax was already well known for its clothing manufacturers. In 1566 there were 2600 inhabitants, making it a fair-sized town at a time when Leeds and Bradford were little more than villages.

A busy market town by the eighteenth century, Halifax had a grim reputation for its public executions: hence the expression 'From Hull, Hell and Halifax Good Lord deliver us!' A replica of the town's guillotine for wrongdoers stands in Gibbet Street. By the nineteenth century Halifax was a busy manufacturing centre, with engineering, wiremaking, sweets (Mackintosh's) and, above all, carpetmaking (Crossley's) supplementing the existing industries.

Superbly situated in a great bowl of hills, traces of old Halifax can still be found in its great parish church (see chapter 5), several older buildings and inns in and around the town centre, and old stony lanes and tracks leading out of the town, including one, the medieval Magna Via, which climbs to the summit of Beacon Hill, the town's ancient beacon.

The most remarkable single building in the town is the Piece Hall (see chapter 8), built in 1775, the great colonnaded cloth market where merchants and clothiers from outlying villages brought their wares. There are also many other fine buildings, mainly Victorian, to explore from the pedestrianised town centre, including the impressive town hall created by Sir Charles Barry (designer of the Houses of Parliament) in 1859, and one of the region's finest Victorian covered markets, all cast iron and glass. Notwithstanding some modern development (and the offices of the nationally known Halifax Building Society are impressive in their own way), Halifax remains one of Britain's finest medium-sized Victorian towns, particularly since the buildings have been cleaned of industrial grime.

There are some interesting things to see in the outskirts, including the gigantic Dean Clough mill complex, one of the largest carpet factories in Europe until its closure some years ago, now returning to life as one of the North's most successful small enterprise and business centres. Shibden Hall and Park (see chapters 6 and 7) form an attractive feature on the east side of the town, whilst to savour the real flavour of old Halifax make your way to the Shears Inn, reached down the cobbled Boys Lane, off Skircoat Road, within a complex of mills and high walls.

You can climb the Wainhouse Tower (reached just off the A646 west of Halifax), a 253 foot (77 metre) high folly, originally built as a chimney for Wainhouse's dyeworks in 1875 and elaborately decorated in a style described by Sir Nikolaus Pevsner as 'flamboyant and fantastical'. Or stroll in the People's Park (just off the A646), a perfect Victorian formal garden laid out in 1856 by Sir Joseph Paxton of Crystal Palace fame. The excellent tourist information centre in the Piece Hall contains details of town walks and trails to explore in this fascinating town.

HAREWOOD

This is the finest example in West Yorkshire of a country estate village. In 1760 it was entirely removed and rebuilt by the Lascelles family of Harewood House outside the walled park at the junction of the new turnpike roads. The houses, handsome stone-built terraces, were designed by John Carr, architect of Harewood House (see chapter 6), for estate managers and workers. The overall effect is of unity and order: a small-scale example of Georgian town planning.

HARTSHEAD

This grey village high above the river Calder was where the young curate Patrick Brontë

The replica of the guillotine at Halifax.

Haworth Parsonage, home of the Brontë family and now a museum.

(there 1811-15) met Miss Branwell: the ensuing family of their marriage was one of the most famous in Yorkshire history. There is a yew tree in its churchyard reputed to be a thousand years old whilst nearby is the elaborately carved stump of Walton Cross, a rare example of a Viking cross.

HAWORTH

World-famous because of its Brontë connections, Haworth retains its early Victorian atmosphere along its celebrated steep cobbled Main Street, now crowded with book and antique shops. You can sit in the public house where Branwell Brontë, assisted by opium, drank himself to an early grave. You can wander down narrow courts and alleyways, past the melancholy graveyard that looms so large in some of Emily's darker poetry.

Alternatively, escape to the beauty of the surrounding moorland, including Penistone Hill Country Park immediately behind the town, where the views across the 'Brontë Moors' are breathtakingly beautiful, particularly in late summer when the heather is reddish-purple. Or you can cross the little park with its bandstand to catch one of the steam trains which at weekends and holiday times chug through Haworth station between Keighley and Oxenhope (see chapter 9). The tourist information centre at the top of Main Street is well supplied with local material. See chapter 7 for the museums.

HEATH

The little village of Heath, about a mile (1.5 km) south-east of Wakefield, is noted for its large village common and magnificent eighteenth-century houses, built for Wakefield merchants. These include Heath House, designed by James Paine (architect of Nostell Priory) and built in the 1740s, and Heath Hall, built by the eminent architect John Carr (designer of Harewood House), who was born in Heath. The King's Arms on the common is noted for its hand-drawn ales served in a tiny gas-lit bar.

HEBDEN BRIDGE

The transformation of Hebden Bridge from a declining textile town to a focal point of West Yorkshire's tourist industry is an intriguing one, which has helped to bring prosperity back to this Pennine community. Its setting is superb: a backcloth of wooded hills up which paths, roads and tracks zigzag, often perilously steeply. Land was so scarce on the valley floor that the characteristic Hebden Bridge 'double-deck' houses were built, terraces built one on top of the other to squeeze them on to the hillside.

The town keeps its original Tudor bridge, its old mills, one of the most perfectly preserved Victorian railway stations in the British Isles, the restored Rochdale Canal with a new marina (see chapter 9), a pleasant town centre park and magnificent scenery all around. The tourist information and exhibition centre is a storehouse of material, with just about every map, booklet and leaflet in print on the whole South Pennines area.

HEPTONSTALL

'The jewel of the South Pennines', Heptonstall is an unspoiled hilltop weavers' settlement high above the Calder Valley (see chapter 8). Notable is the ruined medieval church, roofless and stark, which was simply abandoned to the elements after the new church of St Thomas was built in the 1850s. In the graveyard are many moving memorials, sometimes simple initials of whole young families wiped out in periods of poverty or hardship in the nineteenth century. One gravestone marks the burial place of the notorious David Hartley, one of the Cragg Vale Coiners, hanged at York for clipping gold off sovereigns (a practice which led to the milled edges of today's coins). The celebrated American poetess Sylvia Plath (see chapter 10) is also buried here.

Among the many intriguing buildings is the octagonal Methodist chapel built in 1764 and claimed to be the oldest in continuous use in Britain. There are superb views from the chapel across the Hebden Valley.

HOLME

Holme is a pretty moorland village on the very edge of the Peak District National Park, below Holme Moss Pass. It is close to Digley and Ramsden reservoirs, with attractive picnic sites, woodland and reservoir walks (see chapter 2).

HOLMFIRTH

Market day Thursday.

This small Holme Valley community became famous through the success of the television series *Last of the Summer Wine,* which is filmed in and around the town. Coach parties come to Holmfirth to identify 'Nora Batty's Cottage' and 'Sid's Café' (which has opened as a tea room to satisfy demand, an interesting example of life imitating art).

Television apart, Holmfirth is a fascinating town to explore, with an attractive setting, intriguing and tempting alleyways, a beautiful Georgian church (see chapter 5) and the Postcard Museum (see chapter 7).

HUDDERSFIELD

Market days Monday and Thursday.

Arrive by train in Huddersfield if you can, because the railway station has one of the finest facades of any station in England, with elegantly proportioned colonnades designed by James Pigott of York and built between 1846 and 1850.

The construction of the station was part of the major development of the town in the mid nineteenth century, mainly due to the efforts of the Ramsden family. These were wealthy lords of the manor who had opened the canal to the town in the previous century and who developed the area of handsome buildings around George Square and John William Street. The roots of the town's prosperity lay in the clothing industry, especially fine-quality worsteds for suitings: Huddersfield cloth still has a reputation for being the finest in the world. The town has since diversified into the engineering and chemical industries.

The handsome Italianate town hall, home of the world-famous Huddersfield Choral Society, was built in 1878 and the parish church was rebuilt from a Norman foundation in handsome Perpendicular style in 1836. The town centre has a fine heritage of Victorian buildings, including the restored Byram Arcade, erected in 1880, and the Brook Street Market of 1889. New pedestrianised shopping areas and a covered market make Huddersfield a popular place to shop. There is a tourist information centre in Albion Street, close to

The portico of Huddersfield railway station.

Ilkley in springtime.

the civic buildings.

One of the unacknowledged glories of Huddersfield is its extensive Victorian and Edwardian suburbs, handsome houses in mature gardens which extend up the steep hillsides around the town centre to districts such as Almondbury, Edgerton and Lindley. There are fine parks: Greenhead Park, close to the town centre; Beaumont Park, on the Meltham road, with its impressive views of Lockwood Viaduct on the Penistone Line; and Ravensknowle Park on the Wakefield road, which contains the excellent Tolson Memorial Museum (see chapter 7).

ILKLEY

Though Ilkley's history is ancient (see chapter 3), it remained a relatively small and unimportant village throughout medieval times and into the industrial revolution, when villages like Addingham and Burley and the town of Otley were much more important places. Things changed in the eighteenth century when the fashion grew among the elderly and infirm to take a water cure. This included taking a cold bath and the ice-pure moorland spring which emerges at White Wells on Ilkley Moor was sought after as a remedy for many ailments, including gout. In the 1760s Squire Middleton, the local lord of the manor, authorised the building of the little stone shelter and bath house around the spring, which still stands. By the late eighteenth century people were staying at the lodging houses being built in the little town, to be carried by a donkey up the stony path to White Wells.

The opening in 1843 of Britain's first hydropathic spa at Ben Rhydding near Ilkley, to provide hot and cold water treatment based on the ideas of Dr Preissnitz of Austria, set off a chain reaction of interest. New hydros, offering their patients every luxury (the Victorian equivalent of health farms), followed at Wells House (now Ilkley College) in 1856, Craiglands in 1859, Crossbeck in 1861 and Troutbeck in 1867. The development of the spa town was given new impetus by the opening of the joint Midland and North Eastern Railway in 1865 and soon Ilkley, the 'Malvern of the North', enjoyed a national reputation for the purity of its water, the freshness of its air and the beauty of its scenery.

Inevitably, the new rail services to Leeds and Bradford led to prosperous manufacturers and merchants wanting to bring their families out to live in the peace of Wharfedale, away from the smoky air of the city centres. Handsome villas were therefore built along the hillsides, some of them in grand style. Civic buildings were added: a fine town hall, a library (which now contains the tourist information centre), winter gardens and a concert hall. Various 'walks' were laid out to ensure visitors were entertained and could enjoy the beauties of nature without getting too lost or muddy, both along the riverside and on Ilkley Moor itself, where paths were constructed to two artificial 'tarns' to add interest. Most spectacularly of all, at Heber's Ghyll, about a mile (1.5 km) from the town centre, 'picturesque' walkways were laid out over the natural waterfalls of a moorland stream to give an effect like a Victorian fern garden. This can still be enjoyed, though the many winding steps are hard work for all but the strongest in wind and limb.

Ilkley still retains much of its Victorian and Edwardian charm and attracts visitors in large numbers to enjoy the elegant shops in Brook Street, The Grove or the pedestrianised areas by the main car park, or to wander through its little Victorian arcade, complete with fountain and palms. Even more walk by the river down to the seventeenth-century stone bridge or on to the famous moor. If no one nowadays takes the cure (and the solitary sulphur well in a little park in The Grove has dried up) there are coffee shops, restaurants, concerts in the King's Hall and exhibitions in the Winter Gardens. Yorkshire's Heather Spa remains a delightful place in which to spend leisure time.

KEIGHLEY

Keighley is a busy textile and engineering town at the confluence of the river Aire and the river Worth, which comes down from the Brontë Moors. There is a pleasant town centre: part Victorian, a long shopping street with elegant canopies; part modern, a covered shopping area presided over by a statue of Rombald, the legendary rock-hurling giant of nearby Rombald's Moor. There is a fine park, aviary and museum at Cliffe Castle (see chapter 7), close to the town centre, and the town is the terminus of the Keighley and Worth Valley Railway (chapter 9).

LEEDS

Leeds is West Yorkshire's greatest city, the sixth largest in Britain, with a population of over three-quarters of a million. It is increasingly the administrative, artistic and communications centre of the region.

Though it dates back to iron age times (Loidis was a settlement in the ancient Celtic kingdom of Elmet), the town we see now is relatively modern. Even as late as the sixteenth century it was referred to as 'near Rothwell', a town which is now little more than a suburb of its mighty neighbour.

Leeds grew because of one simple fact: it was the highest point on the river Aire to which a boat could safely be taken. This meant that clothiers could bring their merchandise from outlying towns and villages to sell in Leeds. Initially this took place on Leeds Bridge, as described so graphically by Daniel Defoe in his *Tour through England and Wales* in 1724, close to the wharves on the river Aire. In later years proper trading halls were built: the White Cloth Hall, which was situated where the post office is now (and recalled in the name of the road that leads to it, White Hall Road), whilst the Coloured Cloth Hall still stands, as the classical facade of a plumbers' merchant behind the Corn Exchange.

However, Leeds had always had an important source for a manufacturing tradition: the monks of Kirkstall Abbey, that brilliant and industrious order whose skills as farmers, foresters, tanners, miners and ironmasters survived the Dissolution of the sixteenth century. Kirkstall Forge continued (and continues) an ironmaking and engineering tradition. The skills of a later generation are exemplified by men such as Benjamin Gott, whose Bean Ings factory (established in 1792) became the most prosperous in the region. Gott's grand house and park still survive at Armley as testimony to his success. Between 1770 and 1800 the population of the city had almost doubled from 16,000 to 30,000. By 1850 it had grown fivefold again, to 150,000, and continued to grow fast.

However, Leeds's future lay less in the production of cloth and more in its end use: in clothing. As the city grew it sucked in workers from elsewhere: the Yorkshire Dales, Devon, Scotland, Ireland and Europe. Throughout the nineteenth century, newcomers from eastern Europe, particularly Jewish immigrants, settled in the city and developed Leeds's great tradition of tailoring. This was initially in slum streets and ghetto workshops but, as time passed, workshops and finally factories developed, to create the world's first mass production of ready-made clothing linked to retail outlets. Such household names as Montague Burton and Joseph Hepworth became major enterprises which continue to thrive.

The key to Leeds's success was, and continues to be, diversity. It became a major centre of engineering, with such men as Murray and Blenkinsop creating a tradition for the building of heavy locomotives and traction engines. This was continued by Kitsons (who developed the steam tram), Fowlers (whose great traction engines were seen throughout the world) and the Hunslet Engine Company (whose steam, and latterly diesel, engines are found everywhere). Leeds also developed other skills: printing, street lamps, bootmaking, coachbuilding and service industries. Banking was established with Beckett's Bank (later part of National Westminster) and the Yorkshire Penny Bank (now the Leeds-based Yorkshire Bank).

In 1884 Michael Marks, a Polish-Jewish immigrant, established a penny bazaar in Leeds. This developed into the great chain of Marks and Spencer stores, illustrating the kind of entrepreneurial energy that created Victorian Leeds.

In 1874 the Yorkshire College of Science was founded, soon to be merged with Owen's College, Manchester, and University College, Liverpool, to form the Victoria University. In 1904 Leeds University became independent, a centre for higher education, teaching and research which has a world-wide reputation and has had a major impact on the city.

For all its growth and success in the twentieth century, Leeds remains, in spirit, a late Victorian city. Its great civic buildings include Cuthbert Broderick's massive Town Hall, completed in 1858, a powerful and original building, perhaps Leeds's greatest single piece of architecture. There is also his almost equally impressive Corn Exchange of 1861 and Mechanics' Institute of 1865. Add to that the splendid Venetian-style Market Hall, its great glass roof and wrought iron dragons sheer theatre, City Square itself with Sir Thomas Brock's bronze statue of the Black Prince, surrounded (slightly incongruously) by bronze figures of Night and Day holding their lamps, and the stunningly beautiful and richly decorated Grand Theatre. A series of elegant Victorian and Edwardian arcades all link into a largely pedestrianised town centre. Modern buildings include the 1930s Civic Hall and University, and large shopping centres, offices and banks. However, unlike Bradford, modern development has not been allowed to dominate the centre and what you remember about Leeds is unmistakably Victorian.

Nor has the city been slow to recognise this fact as an advantage. The tourist office runs Victorian weekends to the city, which include visits to the remarkable little City Varieties Theatre on The Headrow. Just round the corner from there, down one of those narrow alleys which evolved out of the medieval town, is Whitelocks, an authentic and unspoiled Victorian public house and dining rooms, which has escaped modernisation to revel in its period charm. Little wonder that Tetley's, the Leeds brewers, produce a regular heritage public house guide which includes beer palaces such as the the Albion on Hunslet Road and the Garden Gate in Hunslet itself.

Many visitors to Leeds have reacted against Leeds's lack of grandeur, noting that it does not have the imposing feel of other great northern cities such as Manchester, Newcastle, Liverpool or even Bradford. That is perhaps true and maybe Leeds remains a small town at heart. It has its compact central shopping centre and its well developed suburbs which are often old townships, like Armley, Headingley, Seacroft and Horsforth, and which keep their own separate identity and character. Also, unlike other cities, the countryside seems to come right into the city centre, with tree-lined roads, open spaces, parks and long strips of woodland. Leeds is a city on a human scale, the central areas, at least, easy to explore on foot.

The parks are truly magnificent. Roundhay Park, with its rose gardens, conservatory, aquarium, lakes and woods, is one of the finest in England. Golden Acre Park has alpine gardens, species roses, an arboretum and a lake rich in wild flowers. Temple Newsam Park is simply the biggest in Europe, while Middleton Park is also immense. Meanwood Park and The Hollies, with their azalea collection, are, in spring, something special.

Leeds is the region's main shopping centre and the city's market is one of the largest in the British Isles, the place where industrial Yorkshire and the rich agricultural Plain of York meet. It is also the region's major cultural and sporting centre, having Opera North, one of Britain's most exciting opera companies, at the Grand Theatre, and Leeds Playhouse, the county's only repertory theatre company. There is a well established season of concerts at the Town Hall, a triennial music festival and the International Pianoforte Competition, as well as a wide choice of popular music and jazz. At Headingley cricket ground, such legendary figures as Sutcliffe, Hutton, Trueman, Close, Illingworth and Boycott learned their trade and test matches are held, whilst Alwoodley has an internationally known golf course.

MARSDEN

The last town in the Colne Valley, Marsden enjoys a superb setting within a bowl of green hills. The little mill town has kept its Victorian flavour, with a fine mechanics' institute and unspoiled shops and cottages. Henrietta Thompson, mother of General James Wolfe, conqueror of Quebec, was a Marsden woman and it is thought that he was born here, in the vicarage. Someone who died here was Enoch Taylor, the Luddite, whose hammer for breaking weaving frames became known as 'Enoch': 'Enoch made 'em, Enoch'll break 'em'. For the Tunnel End Canal and Countryside Centre at Marsden see chapters 2 and 9.

OTLEY

Market days Friday and Saturday.

A medieval market town rich in character and history, Otley has a compact market square out of which a myriad of roads and alleyways lead. It has the flavour of a Dales town, which in effect it is, serving a wide catchment area of mid Wharfedale and Washburndale. There are interesting shops in back streets, old public houses, cafés, workshops, a fine medieval church (see chapter 5) and a popular riverside area with promenades, boating and gardens. The painter J. M. W. Turner spent time in the Otley area when he stayed at Farnley Hall, painting many local landscapes and views for his patrons, the Horton-Fawkes family. The best of these views is undoubtedly from the summit of The Chevin, the great wooded hillside above the town, now forming part of Chevin Forest Park and a short but steep walk from the town centre.

About 3 miles (5 km) from Otley, at White Cross, is Harry Ramsden's, reputedly (and probably) the largest fish and chip shop in the world. This is a fish shop and take-away restaurant which developed in the 1930s from a shed situated close to the tram terminus where waiting passengers could enjoy cheap, hot food. The trams have long gone, but Harry Ramsden's is more popular than ever with a huge car (and coach) park and queues at most times for a characteristic Yorkshire dish.

OXENHOPE

Oxenhope is a compact mill town on the shoulder of the Worth Valley, served by the Keighley and Worth Valley Railway (see chapter 9) and with a sturdy church. It is the starting point for some excellent moorland walks. The village is the setting, every summer, for the Oxenhope Straw Race, a competition between local lads, carrying great bundles of straw on their shoulders, over a difficult course, and the excuse for a major festive occasion in the village.

PONTEFRACT

Market day Saturday.

One of the least known of England's great historical towns, Shakespeare's 'Pomfret', Pontefract owes its existence to the great medieval castle at its eastern end (see chapter 4). The town has winding streets with names that evoke the middle ages: Micklegate, Beast Fair, Corn Market, Shoe Market, Salter Row and Roper Gate. Sadly, decades of insensitive development have masked the old town, but much remains to be discovered for those prepared to look beyond superficial appearances. There are many Georgian houses and shops, and the Buttercross, the focus of a lively street market. There is also an indoor market; the town is a popular shopping centre.

The castle remains the main point of interest in the town but Pontefract's other claim to fame was its liquorice industry. This herb has been grown since monastic times in local fields and even in the ruins of the castle itself. A few roots of the plant are still raised in the local park for the sake of continuity, whilst the famous Pontefract cakes and liquorice allsorts are still made in the locality.

There is a small information centre in the town's museum in Salter Row (see chapter 7).

Ripponden church in winter.

RIPPONDEN

This is a picturesque Pennine town situated in the Ryburn Valley. A fine church, ancient town bridge and compact collection of cottages form the town centre. The bridge, on the site of what was probably a Roman ford, was originally of wood; this was replaced by a stone bridge in 1533. When this was damaged by a flood in 1722 it was replaced by the present stone bridge. The Church Inn by the bridge is at least as old as the bridge itself.

The mills in the Ryburn Valley specialised in the production of dark blue cloth which is said to have once clothed the entire Royal Navy. There is a small information point at Glendale Studio Craft Centre in the parish rooms. The Pennine Farm Museum (see chapter 7) interprets local hill farming in the area.

SOWERBY BRIDGE

Market day Tuesday.

This old textile town owes its prominence to the crossing point over the river Calder utilised by the ancient Chester to York highway. The Calder also provided water power for the early mills, some of which are being restored as part of the Sowerby Bridge Riverside Scheme (see chapter 8). It was also the terminus, transhipment and warehousing point of two canals: the Rochdale and the Calder and Hebble (see chapter 9).

In the fine old church is a statue to Archbishop John Tillotson, born at Old Haugh End House, near to Sowerby Bridge, who became chaplain to King Charles II and later Archbishop of Canterbury. There is an information centre in the main street.

Sowerby Bridge is the setting for one of the region's most important customs, revived in modern times: rushbearing. Rushes were once cut in large numbers as a simple but effective floor covering in country churches. In Sowerby Bridge, on the first weekend in September, bundles of rushes are loaded on to a cart at the Masons' Arms in Warley, a village near Sowerby, and are pulled to St Peter's church and the Star in Sowerby accompanied by brass bands, morris men, dancing and general rejoicing.

STANBURY

A typical moorland village of the Pennines, with gritstone cottages and farms, Stanbury is in a superb setting. It was the home, in the early twentieth century, of Timmy Feather, the last of the Airedale handloom weavers, whose loom and equipment are now kept in Cliffe Castle, Keighley (see chapter 7).

Close by is Ponden Hall, reputedly the setting for Thrushcross Grange in *Wuthering Heights*. It is now a mill shop and craft centre.

TODMORDEN

Market days Wednesday, Friday and Saturday.

Todmorden stands on a crossroads between Lancashire and Yorkshire. Its fine classical town hall has a frieze above its imposing steps depicting local industry: on the western side bales of cotton, on the east wool. At one time the county boundary ran underneath the town hall and a delicate political balance had to be maintained.

For all its position as an outpost of Yorkshire, closer to Burnley or Rochdale than Halifax or Bradford, Todmorden is a thoroughly Yorkshire town, its stone cottages and terraces rising steeply up the hillside, mills and the newly restored Rochdale Canal on the narrow valley floor and superb green hills all around. Centre Vale Park is delightful and extensive, stretching up the valley towards the curiously named village of Portsmouth on the Lancashire boundary.

WAKEFIELD

West Yorkshire's and the West Riding's old county town might have been robbed of its former importance, but its position, on the foothills of the Pennines overlooking the softer countryside of the north Midlands, and its excellent communications, with the M1 and M62 motorways and the newly electrified East Coast main line, ensure its continued prosperity and importance.

It is the only one of the larger West Yorkshire towns to have been an important centre in Anglo-Saxon times. Built on a hill above the Calder where the three main streets of Westgate, Northgate and Kirkgate still run, it had strategic importance at the time of the Wars of the Roses. When the Duke of York was defeated at the battle of Wakefield in 1460 it gave rise to the nursery rhyme 'The Grand Old Duke of York'. Wakefield also has Robin Hood associations: according to Wakefield Court Rolls Robin lived in the town before fleeing after the battle of Boroughbridge to become an outlaw. The town was notorious for a time in the early nineteenth century because of the activities of 'Resurrectionists', body snatchers who stole corpses from graveyards for medical research.

The modern city, close to the great Yorkshire coalfield, is an important industrial and administrative town but keeps something of its former elegance in attractive areas of Georgian and Regency terraces and squares, particularly around St John's church. There are fine civic buildings too, notably the Town Hall, the County Courts and the massive County Hall, a building of richly decorated interiors which, as the former administrative headquarters of England's largest county, West Riding, still seeks a future. The town centre is dominated by the cathedral with its elegant spire (see chapter 5) and a superb shopping centre.

The Ridings Shopping Centre differs from almost any other in England by virtue of the imaginative way it has been developed. It exploits its hillside site, with different levels of shops and car park linked by an astonishing illuminated glass lift, and attractive greenhouse-style gardens and eating areas, exhibition and display spaces. It has won a number of top European prizes and is well worth a visit.

Wakefield's advantage is its compactness, with convenient train and bus stations and car parking areas close to the pedestrianised shopping streets and lively market. As well as excellent art galleries and museum (see chapter 7), there is the reopened Theatre Royal and Opera House on Westgate and, for real ale enthusiasts, also on Westgate, Henry Boon's cleverly restored Victorian public house selling Clarke's excellent Wakefield-brewed ale.

WETHERBY

Market day Thursday.

Perhaps West Yorkshire's most charming country market town, Wetherby, now avoided by the A1, has a rural ambience, which owes more to the nearby Plain of York than to the Pennines. It once had a castle, built by the Knights Templar in the eleventh century, only a few stones of the foundations of which remain, whilst the great weir across the river Wharfe is reputed to be medieval, providing water power for a mill. The soft cream stone of its Georgian houses and shops, its early Victorian town hall and lovely old bridge over the river Wharfe make Wetherby a pleasant town in which to stroll. There are a handsome church of the 1830s, interesting shops (both traditional and along a new shopping mall), racing on the nearby racecourse and attractive countryside all around. There is a tourist information centre in the town hall.

12
Getting around

It is easy to get to West Yorkshire by road, rail or air. The M1 and M62 motorways and the A1(M) trunk road serve the county, providing fast, easy travel by car and coach from the South-east, the North-west and from the port of Hull, with its overnight boats from Holland and Belgium.

Inter-City high-speed electric trains arrive at Wakefield and Leeds every hour from London, whilst Birmingham and the Midlands also have frequent services. There is a half-hourly express diesel train from Manchester, as well as services from Scotland, including the dramatically beautiful Leeds-Settle-Carlisle line through the Yorkshire Dales.

Once in Leeds, the West Yorkshire rail network, MetroTrain, links most of the larger towns with speedy trains. Indeed, public transport in West Yorkshire is so good, it can truly be said that this is one of the few regions in Britain in which you do not need to have a car. A network of over fifty local rail stations and interconnecting buses, which operate deep into the hinterland, mostly on a surprisingly regular basis, make all but the most complex journeys relatively easy. There is a lot to be said for leaving a car outside towns such as Leeds and Bradford and coming into the centres by bus or train. With cheap off-peak (after 9.30 am and weekends) fares, it is often less expensive than parking, whilst the 'Go Anywhere' Day Rover bus and rail pass, offering unlimited travel in West Yorkshire, represents extremely good value for money for anyone wanting to discover the county. Holders of the ticket can often get discounted admission to local tourist attractions.

Leeds-Bradford Airport has frequent shuttle flights to and from London Heathrow, as well as to other British destinations and to Amsterdam. The airport is about 10 miles (16 km) from the centre of Leeds and 7 miles (11 km) from Bradford.

13
Tourist information centres

Bradford: City Hall, Bradford BD1 1HY. Telephone: 0274 753678.

Halifax: Piece Hall, Halifax HX1 1RE. Telephone: 0422 68725.

Hartshead Moor Service Area (M62): Clifton, near Brighouse HD6 4JX. Telephone: 0274 869167. On westbound service area; access from eastbound carriageway by pedestrian overbridge

Haworth: 2/4 West Lane, Haworth, Keighley BD22 8EF. Telephone: 0535 42329.

Hebden Bridge: 1 Bridge Gate, Hebden Bridge HX7 9JP. Telephone: 0422 843831.

Holmfirth: 49/51 Huddersfield Road, Holmfirth. Telephone: 0484 684992 or 687603.

Huddersfield: 3/5 Albion Street, Huddersfield HD1 2NW. Telephone: 0484 22133 or 23877 (Saturdays).

Ilkley: Station Road, Ilkley LS29 8HA. Telephone: 0943 602319.

Leeds: 19 Wellington Street, Leeds LS1 4DG. Telephone: 0532 462454.

Otley: 8 Boroughgate, Otley LS21 3AH. Telephone: 0943 465151.

Wakefield: Town Hall, Wood Street, Wakefield WF1 2HQ. Telephone: 0924 370211 extension 7021 or 7022 (office hours); 370700 (outside office hours).

Wetherby: Council Offices, 24 Westgate, Wetherby LS22 4NL. Telephone: 0937 62706.

WEST YORKSHIRE
⊓ Archaeological site (Ch.3)
C Castle or fortification (Ch.4)
A Abbey (Ch.4)
+ Church (Ch.5)
▲ Historic house or garden (Ch.6)
M Museum (Ch.7)
I Industrial history (Ch.8)
■ Town or village (Ch.11)
Addingham
ILKLEY
Ilkley Moor
KEIGHLEY
East Riddlesden Hall
Micklethwaite
Baildon Moor
Goose Eye
Holden Park
BINGLEY
Keighley & Worth Valley Railway
Saltaire
Stanbury
Haworth
Oxenhope
BRADFORD
Bolling Hall
M606
Heptonstall
Hebden Bridge
Mount Cross
Shibden Hall
HALIFAX
TODMORDEN
Te Deum Stone
Sowerby Bridge
BRIGHOUSE
Lumbutts and Mankinholes
Clay House
Elland
Ripponden
M62
Colne Valley Museum
HUDDERSF
R.Colne
Castle Hill
Marsden Moor
Marsden
Jack Metcalfe's Turnpike
Meltham
Holmfirth
Holme

Wetherby
R. Wharfe
Boston Spa
Harewood
Clifford
Bramhope
Bardsey
Bramham
Bramham Park
Adel
Meanwood Park
Kirkstall Abbey
Kirkstall Valley
Aberford
Lotherton Hall
LEEDS
Whitkirk
Farnley Park
Temple Newsam House
Fulneck
Middleton Railway
Thwaites Mill
Tong-Cockersdale
M621
R. Aire
Ledsham
M62
R. Calder
CASTLEFORD
M1
BATLEY
DEWSBURY
PONTEFRACT
WAKEFIELD
Heath
West Hardwick
Sandal Castle
Nostell Priory
Ackworth
Yorkshire Mining Museum
Badsworth
Yorkshire Sculpture Park
Denby Dale

Index

Page numbers in italic refer to illustrations.

Abbey House Museum 14, 29
Aberford 9, 12, 41
Ackworth 10, 41
Addingham 10, 16, 32
Addingham High Moor 10, 11, 12
Adel 9, 16
Adwalton Moor *3*
Aire and Calder Navigation 35
Airedale 6, 36, 41
Almondbury 11, 48
Alwoodley 9, 50
Armley Mills 30
Asquith, Herbert 40
Automobilia 28
Badsworth 10, 41
Bagshaw Museum 25, 41, *41*
Baildon 6, 40
Baildon Moor 6, *11,* 12
Bankfield Museum 27
Bardsey 16, 39, 41
Barstow, Stan 40
Batley 25, 40, 41, *41*
Becca Banks 12
Ben Rhydding 48
Bentley, Phyllis 33, 39
Bingley 6, 10, 36, 40, 41-2, *42*
Birstall 23, 40
Blackstone Edge 7, 8, 12
Blenkinsop, John 38, 40, 49
Bolling Hall 20, *20*
Boston Spa 9, 10, 42
Bracken Hall 6
Bradford 3, 6, 16, *16,* 20, *20,* 25, 26, 36, 37, 38, 39, 40, 42-4, *43*
Braine, John 40
Bramham 44
Bramham Park 20
Bramhope 16, 18, 38
Bretton Park 9
Brighouse 26, 36, 44
Brontë Country/Moors 3, 6, 39, 46
Brontë family 6, 23, 28, 37, 39, *39,* 44, 45-6
Brontë Parsonage Museum 28, 39, *46*
Calder and Hebble Navigation 34, 35-6, 37, 44, 51
Calderdale 3, 6, 6-8, 37, 39
Calderdale Industrial Museum 27
Calderdale Pre-industrial Museum 27
Calderdale Way 7, 8, 13
Canals 35-7
Caphouse Colliery 34
Cartwright Hall 25, *26*
Castleford 12, 26, 40
Castle Hill 11
Chevin 9, 10, 51
Chippendale, Thomas 21, 22, 23, 40, *40*
Civil War 3, 14, 15, 16, 20, 42
Clay House 8, 21
Cliffe Castle 29
Clifford 9, 17
Cliviger Gorge 7, 12, 38
Clogmaking 28
Cockcroft, Sir John 40
Colne Valley 6, *8,* 8-9, 33, 36, 50
Colne Valley Museum 27
Colour Museum 26
Congreve, William 39
Cow and Calf Rocks *10,* 12
Cullingworth 6
Cup and ring stones 11-12, *13*
Dales Way 10
Darnley, Lord 24
Delius, Frederick 40, 43
Denby Dale 44
Dewsbury 17, 26, *27,* 44-5
Disraeli, Benjamin 6
Druids Altar 6
Eastergate Bridge 12
East Riddlesden Barn 12
East Riddlesden Hall 21
Ebor Way 10
Elizabethan Exhibition Gallery 30
Elland 36, 44
Fairburn Ings 9
Farnley Park 21
Fulneck Moravian Museum 27
Gibson Mill 7
Golcar 27
Golden Acre Park 9, 50
Gomersal 23, 41
Goose Eye 44
Green Crag Slack 12
Grimsworth Dean 7, 32
Guiseley 38
Halifax 3, 6, 17, 27, *32,* 33-4, 35, 36, 38, 45, *45*
Piece Hall 27, *32,* 33-4, 45
Hardcastle Crags 6, 7, 32
Harewood 9, 10, 45
Harewood Castle 14
Harewood House *21,* 21-2, 40
Harry Ramsden's 51
Hartshead 45-6
Hawksworth Moor 12
Haworth 6, *37,* 38, 39, 46, *46*
Headingley 9, 38, 50
Heath 46
Hebden Bridge 6, 7, 28, 33, 37, 46-7
Heber's Ghyll 12, 49
Heptonstall 7, 28, 32, 40, 47
Hepworth, Barbara 30, 40
Hockney, David 40
Holbeck 40
Holden Park 22
Hollies, The 22, 50
Holme 9, 47
Holme Valley 9, 38, 44, 47
Holmfirth 9, 17, 28, 47
Hood, Robin 52
Horses at Work 27-8
Horsforth 38, 50
Hoyle, Sir Fred 40
Huddersfield 3, 6, 11, 28, 36, 40, *47,* 47-8
Huddersfield Broad Canal 36
Huddersfield Narrow Canal *35,* 36
Hughes, Ted 39
Ilkley 9, 10, 12, *13, 17,* 17-18, 28, *29,* 38, *48,* 48-9
Ilkley Moor 10, *10,* 11-12, 40, 49
Jack Metcalfe's Turnpike Road 32
Keighley 10, 29, 37, 38, 49
Keighley and Worth Valley Railway *37,* 38, 40, 49, 51
Kirkstall Abbey 14, *15,* 29, 49
Kirkstall Valley 32
Last of the Summer Wine 47
Ledsham 9, 18
Leeds *1, 2,* 3, 4, 6, 9, 14, 18, 29-30, 35, 36, 37, 38, 40, 49-50
Civic Hall *2,* 50
Town Hall *1,* 50
University 50
Leeds and Liverpool Canal 29, 36, 42
Leeds Country Way 9
Lister Park 25
Lister's Mill 43, *43*
Lotherton Hall 22
Luddenden Dean 7
Luddenden Foot 6
Luddites 32-3, 39
Lumbutts 7, 33
Mankinholes 7, 33
Manningham 43, *43*
Manor House Museum 12, 28, *29*
Marks and Spencer 49
Marsden 8, *35,* 36, 50
Marsden Moor 33
Meanwood Park 22, 50
Meanwood Valley Trail 9, 22
Meltham 18
Metcalfe, Jack 32
Micklefield 38
Micklethwaite 33
Middleton Lodge 12
Middleton Railway 38
Middleton Woods 9
Mirfield 36
Morley 40
Moore, Henry 29, 30, 31, 40
Moorside Mill 25, *25*
Mount Cross 12
Murray, Matthew 38, 40, 49
Museum of Childhood 28
Mytholmroyd 6, 37, 39
National Museum of Photography, Film and Television 26
Newmillerdam 9
North Dean 8, 21
Nostell Priory 9, *22,* 22-3, 40
Nutclough Mill 33
Oakwell Hall 23, *23*
Ossett 40
Otley 9, 10, 18, 30, 40, *40,* 50-1
Oxenhope 6, 38, 51
Paulinus, St 44
Peak District 5, 8-9, 47
Penistone Hill 6, 46
Pennine Farm Museum 30
Pennines 3, 4, 5, 6, 7, 8, 9, 32, 36, 37, 52
Pennine Way 6, 7
Plath, Sylvia 39, 47
Pontefract 14, 18, 30, 51
Priestley, J. B. 39
Priestley, Joseph 40
Railways 37-8, 53
Red House 23, *24*
Rein, The 12
Richard II 15
Ringstone Edge 11
Ripponden 8, 11, 30, *51*
Rochdale Canal 34, 36-7, 46, 51, 52
Roman roads 12
Rombalds Moor 10, 49
Roundhay 9, 50
Rushbearing 52
Ryburn Valley 8, 51
St Ives Estate 6, 42
Salt, Sir Titus *33,* 34
Saltaire 6, 30, 33, 34, 36, 38, 43
Salterhebble 36
Sandal Castle *14,* 15, 31
Scammonden Reservoir 8
Seacroft 9, 50
Shibden 23, 30
Shibden Hall 23-4, 30, 45
Shipley 6, 36, 37
Shipley Glen Rocks 11
Shipley Glen Tramway 6, 38
Shoddy 41, 44
Silsden 10, 36
Smeaton, John 19, 40, 44
Smith Art Gallery 26, 44
Soldier's Edge 12
Sowerby Bridge 6, 34, 35, 36, 37, 51-2
Spen Valley 33, 39
Stanbury *5,* 6, 52
Standedge 8, 32, 33, *35,* 36
Stoodley Pike 7
Street Farm 12
Summit Gap 7
Swastika Stone 10, 12
Te Deum Stone 13
Temple Newsam 9, 24, 50
Thornton *39,* 39
Thorpe Arch 42
Thwaites Mill 34
Todmorden 6, 7, 36-7, 37, 38, 40, 52
Tolson Memorial Museum 11, 28
Tong-Cockersdale 9, 34
Top Farm Agricultural Museum 31
Top Withins 6, 39
Tunnel End Canal and Countryside Centre 8, 33, *35,* 36
Turner, J. M. W. 50
Twelve Apostles 12
Victoria Reed Organ Museum 30
Wainhouse Tower 45
Wakefield 3, 9, 12, 15, 19, 30-1, 35, 37, 40, 52
battle 15, 52
Bridge Chapel 19, *19*
Walkley's Clog Mill 28
Warley 52
Wentbridge 9, 10
Wessenden Valley 8
West Hardwick 31
West Vale 8, 21
West Yorkshire Folk Museum 30
West Yorkshire Transport Museum 26
Wetherby 9, 52-3
Wharfedale 6, 10, 38, 48, 50
White House Information Centre 9
White Wells 10, 12, 48
Whitkirk 19
Wilson, Harold 40
Windgate Nick 10
Wintersett Reservoir 9
Worth Valley *5,* 6, 38, 49, 51
Wragby church 23
Wuthering Heights 6, 39, 52
Yorkshire Dales 5, 10, 38
Yorkshire Mining Museum 34
Yorkshire Sculpture Park 9, 31, *31,* 40